A Ray of Light

A Ray of Light

Instructions on Piety, the Passions, and the End Times

Compiled by
Archimandrite Panteleimon (Nizhnik)

Translated by Michael Hilko

Holy Trinity Publications
The Printshop of St Job of Pochaev
Holy Trinity Monastery
Jordanville, New York
2024

A Ray of Light © 1991 Holy Trinity Monastery
Revised Text: A Ray of Light © 2024 Holy Trinity Monastery
First printing (in Russian): 1946 at Holy Trinity Monastery

PRINTSHOP OF
SAINT JOB OF POCHAEV

An imprint of

HOLY TRINITY PUBLICATIONS
Holy Trinity Monastery
Jordanville, New York 13361-0036
www.holytrinitypublications.com

ISBN: 978-0-88465-507-7 (paperback)
ISBN: 978-0-88465-513-8 (ePub3)

Library of Congress Control Number: 2024942548

Cover: Interior of Holy Trinity Cathedral, Jordanville, New York.

New Testament Scripture passages taken from the New King James Version.
Copyright © 1982 by Thomas Nelson, Inc. Used by permission.
Psalms taken from A Psalter for Prayer, trans. David James
(Jordanville, N.Y.: Holy Trinity Publications, 2011).
Old Testament and Apocryphal passages taken from the Orthodox Study Bible.
Copyright © 2008 by Thomas Nelson, Inc. Used by permission.

Contents

Preface   vii

1   A Ray of Light: How to Leave the Darkness of
Death. The Perception of Truth   1

2   What Will Be the Status of the Incomplete
Blessedness of Righteous Souls and the
Incomplete Torture of Sinful Souls?   7

3   The Fate in the Future Life of Sinful People,
Unrepentant of Their Sins   12

4   The Incorruptibility and Miraculous Powers
of Holy Relics   19

5   The Veneration of Holy Icons   21

6   Christ's Holy Church   24

7   The Characteristics of People before the End
of the World. A Prophecy   31

8   Apostasy in the Last Days of the World   35

9   Signs by Which the Nearness of the Second
Coming of Jesus Christ Can Be Judged   45

10   The Coming of the Antichrist   48

11   The Birth of Antichrist and His Acceptance
by the Jews as the True Messiah   53

12   The Antichrist Foretold   55

13   The Actions and the Name of the Antichrist   56

14	The Seal of Antichrist	59
15	The Miracles of the Antichrist	61
16	The Disparagement of Divine Law by the Antichrist; The Persecutions and Tortures of Those Confessing Christ	64
17	The Construction by the Antichrist of His Altar in the Temple at Jerusalem	66
18	The Terrible State of the World and All Mankind during the Reign of the Antichrist	68
19	Posthumous Prophecies of Our Holy Father Nilus the Myrrh-streamer of Mount Athos	72
20	The Word of Our Holy Father Ephraim the Syrian on the Coming of the Antichrist	93

Appendix: A Short Biography of Archimandrite Panteleimon (Nizhnik) — 107

Notes — 109

Preface

In the matter of salvation, the understanding of the truth is indispensable; without it no one can achieve eternal life. It is said that they who are strangers to the illumination of truth "walk as the rest of the Gentiles walk, in the futility of their mind, having their understanding darkened, being alienated from the life of God" (Eph 4:17–18); "who have their portion in this life" (Ps 17:14 NKJV); "whose end is destruction, whose god is their belly, and whose glory is in their shame—who set their mind on earthy things" (Phil 3:19). The truth of God calls such people a "faithless and perverse generation" (Matt 17:17), and for that reason says to us: "Be saved from this perverse generation" (Acts 2:40). And so, man, life and death are up to you. Select whichever you want; search for what is better for you—to remain now in spiritual darkness and the shadow of death (see Matt 4:16), and then to go to eternal suffering, or to turn from evil and enter the ever-present life and light—to "inherit the kingdom prepared for you from the foundation of the world" (Matt 25:34). And so?—"that light has come into the world," says the Lord, "and men loved darkness rather than light" (John 3:19). The prophets, too, appealed: "O Lord, who has believed our report, and to whom was the arm of the Lord revealed?" (Isa 53:1) "You are mistaken, not knowing the Scriptures nor the power of God" (Matt 22:29). These are the main barriers to our enlightenment and achievement of eternal life, i.e., not knowing the scriptures, nor the power of God.

A sharp sword is handy and even necessary while traveling, or where danger abounds, since with its help one can defend oneself from enemies; but it often leads also to destruction, serving as the instrument for robberies, threats, and murders. Like this sword, reflection and investigation concerning the time for the ending of the world is beneficial for people to the same degree that it is harmful. Judicious and worthy of praise is he, who, while dwelling mentally on the immensity of the almightiness and justice of God, does not forget his own personal demise, remembers that in the future he will receive the recompense for his deeds, becomes fearful of eternal sufferings, and directs his efforts toward good works.

In presenting this book to the reader we, with God's help, have decided to reveal the true signs of the coming of the Antichrist which will occur before the world's end. This is especially important for ordinary people, who, like leaves, waver in their understanding about the Antichrist, credulously blown about, accepting various false explanations.

Devout reader! Accept without fear the spiritual food offered by this book; forsake all doubts, for you can be assured that everything we speak of will be founded on the Word of God and the interpretations of the holy and God-fearing Fathers and teachers of the Church: John Chrysostom, Andrew of Caesarea, John of Damascus, Ephraim the Syrian, Cyril of Jerusalem, Nilus of the Holy Mountain, Bishop Theophan the Recluse, Bishop Ignatius Brianchaninov, our Father John of Kronstadt, the Miracle-Worker, and others.

We have not dared to resolve the higher and unattainable mysteries of God, leaving this right to the One Divine Church, which has eagle's wings. "But the woman was given two wings of a great eagle" (Rev 12:14), says the seer of mysteries. "The holy Church was given the godly wisdom of two testaments," the holy Fathers relate—guided aloft by these two wings we have written this book to first quiet the lips of false teachers, and, secondly, to furnish pious people with useful and soul-saving reading material.

Let all of this be in honor and praise of our Lord God, Who punishes us with His righteous judgment. He, the All-just, permits confusion and discord in the Church, in order to cleanse His selected ones in the refinery of temptations like gold. He produces storms and subdues the winds and storms of the seas. He never leaves His Church unguarded, but directs it amid powerful, beastly, worldly misfortunes, and steers it to a peaceful harbor.

The Abbot of the Holy Trinity Monastery
January 16, 1946, Abbot Panteleimon

CHAPTER ONE

A Ray of Light: How to Leave the Darkness of Death. The Perception of Truth

Infinitely great, incomprehensible, and ineffable is God's love for sinful mankind! For the salvation of mankind, He sent to earth His Only-begotten Son, Who, taking on a servant's appearance, became a man similar to us and during a span of thirty-three and a half years lived among sinful people and served them, instructing them in true God-pleasing life.

Though without stain of sin, He took upon Himself the sins of mankind, through His unutterable love toward the race of man, undergoing for them grievous suffering and agonizing death on a cross of wood. He then descended into hell with His soul, and there defeated the sovereignty of the devil, thereby reconciling us with God and opening to us access to eternal blessedness in the heavenly Kingdom. But this is not all! Knowing that people, because of their sinful nature, cannot by their own efforts obtain the saving fruits of redemption, He also provided the means for salvation—He founded here the holy Church, or His Kingdom. On the tenth day after His ascension into heaven, He sent the apostles His Holy Spirit, Who perpetually resides in the Church and covers all its members, helping them to save themselves in Christ. In this way, the Lord accomplishes for us everything which one can desire; He gave us all the tools necessary for salvation. It depends only on us—to use or not to use these means.

Having granted us the means of achieving salvation, the Lord also designated a fixed term, during which we can make use of these means. For each of us, this term ends along with our earthly life, and for all mankind it ends with the end of the world. But you, brethren, must know that with the death of the body, life does not end; our bodies die, but our immortal souls continue to exist. In the same way the life of the whole race of man will not end with the end of the world. After the general resurrection a new life will begin, "the life of the future age." At our own death, therefore, the matter of our salvation will not be ended. The Lord will judge us, weighing correctly whether we made use of the means given us for salvation and are worthy of eternal blessedness.

Having passed judgment, He shall reward us justly. To each, according to his merits, He shall determine our destiny in eternal life. Judgment and recompense will complete the matter of salvation effected by the Lord. The Orthodox Church differentiates between the two judgments of God. There is a private trial for every person separately, and a general trial for the whole race of mankind.

The private trial and judgment of one's soul begins immediately after a person's death. "And as it is appointed for men to die once, but after this the judgement," says the holy Apostle Paul (Heb 9:27). This private trial is held for every person, since all people, as descendants of Adam, who sinned and was judged, are sinful and must face God's judgment. Besides, since death entered through sin, death is the unavoidable consequence and result of sin. Death consists of the separation of the soul and body: "Then the dust returns to the earth as it was, and the spirit returns to God who gave it" (Eccl 12:7). This spirit will remain alive and immortal, going on to face the private judgment of God immediately after the death of the body.

Holy Scripture does not discuss the private judgment of God. We know of this judgment from Church Tradition, preserved in the writings of its holy teachers. According to the teaching of the Church, this judgment will take place in the following manner. Picture a dying person; just as at the birth of a person into the world, relatives meet and receive into their arms the new little member of this earth, so, the soul, upon separation from the body, as if being born into another world, is met and received by bodiless spirits, the inhabitants of the spiritual world beyond the grave. At the moment of death, good spirits, the holy angels, with our guardian angel at the head, will appear on one side, and on the other side will be wicked spirits, devils, "the rulers of the darkness of this age" (Eph 6:12). Seeing the wicked spirits, the soul of the person is troubled, alarmed, and struck with dismay, and looks to the angels of God for help. This is the reason for those striking scenes which are often observed at the bedsides of the dying. The latter seems to be turning away from one side in terror, and then turns to the other side in indescribable happiness. We think that these are the nightmares of a sick imagination. No. The dying person sees the devils on one side and the angels on the other. St Ephraim the Syrian says, "When the ruling powers approach the dying person, and when the godly messengers order the soul to leave the body, then, seeing them, the poor person trembles like a leaf shaken by the wind, struggles like a swallow in the hands of the hunter, is numbed and surprised, seeing the terrible powers, seeing majestic images new to him, seeing an order of things which he never saw before." And the poor soul sees who of the bodiless spirits attending it has more power over it, the angels or the devils. If, while living on earth, it followed the advice of the devil, it is even more dismayed and worried; if the suggestions of the angels were its rules of life, it is soothed. And here the word of God is justified—"the death of sinners is severe, *while* the death of the upright is honorable; and when death overtakes the righteous, he will be at rest."

Having parted from the body, the soul appears for God's judgment, which is accomplished by angels at the so-called toll house trials. In order to rise up to God, the soul must pass through these trials, which as St Cyril of Jerusalem describes, "are like unto toll-gates or examination rooms, where it [the soul] is questioned and tried for the deeds of its earthly life." It will meet the inquisitors and torturers (devils), who during our lives participated in our evil deeds, aroused in us sinful thoughts and desires, and hindered our performance of good deeds. They, as witnesses of the sinful side of our life, will be the accusers of the soul in its trials. These horrible beings meet the soul, examine the record, and note and describe in detail all the sins of the soul—sins of youth and age, voluntary and involuntary, committed in deed or by word or only in thought—and great is the terror and fear of the poor soul; indescribable the grief which the soul suffers then from the enemies surrounding it, slandering it in order not to allow it to rise to heaven to take up its abode in the land of life.

On the other side the bright angels together with our guardian angels will appear as the defenders of our souls. As our witnesses and helpers in our pure and holy deeds, thoughts, and desires, they will seek out our good deeds to justify us before the court of God's truth. There will be a special trial for every sin and passion of our soul, so that for every sin there will be a special ordeal. There will be twenty such ordeals, as it was disclosed to St Gregory, the pupil of the holy monk Basil the New. At the first ordeal the sins of the mouth and tongue will be the subjects of the inquisition; for instance, idle talk, profanity, rowdiness, lying, calumny, and so forth; at the second—sins of vision; at the third—sins of hearing, and so forth. Further ordeals will be for the sins of anger, rage, malice, loathing, jealousy, pride, greed, lust, heresies, schisms, and others. At all of these ordeals, the tormenting spirits of malice will remind the poor soul of every occurrence in its life—of where and when it was implicated in one or another sin—and will point out in detail the time and scene of our evil doings. The poor soul will flutter in fright and prayerfully look toward the angels of God. They, our guardians (about whom in the course of our lives we often forget), will defend the soul, pointing out when and where it performed good deeds. And this will be the time for remembering before God "the cup of cool water," given in the name of Christ (see Mark 9:41), and the "tear drop," and even "part of a tear" shed for our iniquities; also remembered will be every prayerful sigh sent to God from the depths of a humble and contrite heart.

Such will be the personal judgment of the soul of every man. Of course it will be accomplished by the Lord God, Himself, but it will be carried out by His angels, in the presence of demons. Take note, brethren, this will be a real trial. Here will be found the accusers of a man, demons; and his defenders, the holy angels. Nothing will be concealed here; the judgment will be just and impartial.

Just as at earthly trials people are exonerated or condemned, so will it be at the personal judgment of God. After the trial the Lord will determine the fate of each person. If one acted right-eously and piously while living on earth, his soul is carried up by holy angels to a place of joy and blessedness. If, however, the ordeals prove that the person passed his life in negligence and incontinence, in vices and dishonesty, then, according to the condemnation of the Judge, his soul is given into the power of the demons and they drag the poor thing into a dreary, dark region, settling it in a place of sorrow and sighing.

However, it must be noted that the recompense which is received by both sinners and the just after the personal judgment is not complete. The holy Fathers teach that souls, having parted from their bodies, though they soon pass either to happiness or to sorrow and grief, do not yet feel either total blessedness or complete suffering. For everyone will receive full blessedness, or full suffering, only after the general resurrection, when the soul will be reunited with the body. This will occur after the Second Coming into the world of the Lord Jesus Christ, and after the Last Judgment.

In the future life, man will receive recompense for his earthly actions. Man lives on earth, either saving himself or sinning, by means of not only his soul, but the body too. This means that complete recompense must be received by the complete man, composed of soul and body. The body of man must share either in blessedness, or in suffering, just as on earth, it, together with the soul, deserved one and the same fate. All of this will be achieved only after the general resurrection of the dead and after Christ's Last Judgment.

CHAPTER TWO

What Will Be the Status of the Incomplete Blessedness of Righteous Souls and the Incomplete Torture of Sinful Souls?

The souls of the righteous are carried by angels to the place of blessedness, which in God's holy Scripture is called paradise, Abraham's bosom, the heavenly Kingdom, God's Kingdom, the house of the heavenly Father, heavenly Jerusalem, and so forth. While situated here, the righteous souls reside at rest from all toil, in a place where there is no sickness, sorrow, or sighing. They are in close communion with other righteous souls and with angels, in the sight of God, anticipating that eternal blessedness, which we cannot now even begin to imagine for ourselves.

But, just as not all holy people are equally righteous and virtuous, so the blessed state of souls in heaven will have various degrees. "In My Father's house are many mansions," Jesus Christ said (John 14:2). The Apostle Paul adds that every man shall receive his own reward according to his own labor (see 1 Cor 3:8). The degree of blessedness will correspond to the degree of the deeds—what we shall sow here on earth, that we shall reap in heaven.

The glorification of the righteous is not limited only to the heavenly mansions. Our Lord, the just Judge and Giver of gifts, also glorifies His saints in the earthly Church. This glorification, according to the instructions of the Church, consists of our revering the departed righteous ones as saints and friends of God, as "the speedy helpers and intercessors for my soul,"[1] venerating their incorrupt relics and their icons.

We call the righteous departed, saints of God, in the sense that they pleased God in their life, and for that reason were worthy to receive eternal blessedness. But, revering saints of God, we do not place them on the same level with the Lord God, nor regard them as gods, but accept them as true servants of God, friends of God. These words are often heard in Church: "Wonderful is God in His saints" (Ps 67:36 LXX), meaning that God is glorified through His saints. Living on earth, they praised God's name by their life of righteousness, glorifying the name of the heavenly Father, and now, residing in heaven, God's name is praised through their memory among people. Therefore, revering God's righteous people, we honor in them God Himself, Whom they pleased while on earth, and Whose grace resides in them. The Saviour, while regarding as His friends all those who fulfilled His commandments, said to His disciples: "He who receives you receives Me, and he who receives Me receives Him who sent Me" (Matt 10:40). Our Lord is clearly showing that the honor rendered to His faithful servants and friends is imputed to Himself.

How can we not venerate the saintly and righteous, who were glorified by the Lord God Himself?! We respect people whose services and feats are rewarded by an earthly king; all the more we should venerate the saints who were exalted by the heavenly King. We honor earthly kings' servants in a worldly manner: we meet them triumphantly, honor them with banquets, remember them with expensive statues; but the saintly righteous ones we revere spiritually. In their honor we arrange annual church holidays, glorify them in hymns, build temples and chapels in their honor, imitate their exploits, and so forth. All of these celebrations began from the first centuries of Christianity, as church history witnesses. Revering the saints as faithful servants and friends of God, we also appeal to them in our prayers. We cry out, "Pray to God for us, you righteous of God, for we diligently have recourse to you, who help us and pray for our souls." From this prayerful supplication, it can be seen that we do not regard the saintly and righteous as gods, and do not think that they by their own personal power assist us in our needs. No—they are only intercessors, our pleaders before God, who can assist us only by their prayers.

There is no doubt that the Lord Himself immediately hears the prayers of all individuals, but our innumerable sins interfere with the power of our prayers. "Now we know that God does not hear sinners," said the one who though blind from birth was cured by the Saviour, "but if anyone is a worshiper of God and does His will, He hears him" (John 9:31). However, the holy saints of God, by their exploits, earned for themselves God's eternal good will, and for this reason the Lord listens to their prayers for us sinners.

Standing before the altar of the heavenly King, they seem to personally transmit to Him our needs and sorrows. And great is the power of their intercession: "The effective, fervent prayer of a righteous man avails much," the Apostle James teaches us (Jas 5:16).

How can we not appeal in prayer to the saintly righteous ones, who have already entered the heavenly mansions, when we know that even while living on earth they had the power to intercede before God for sinful people? God Himself commanded a king to entreat the righteous Abraham to pray for him, saying: "For he is

a prophet; and he will pray for you, and you shall live" (Gen 20:7);
The Lord commanded the friends of the long-suffering Job, who
had offended him, to ask his prayers: "go to my servant Job … and
my servant Job shall pray for you. For I will only accept him, but
for his sake, I would have destroyed you" (Job 42:8). Because of
the prayers of the righteous, the Lord often spared people who
had sinned. Moses prayed for the Hebrew people who had fallen
into the sin of idol worship and were already doomed to destruction by God; the Lord accepted the prayer of the holy man and
pardoned the stiff-necked people (see Exod 32:9–12). The Lord
once said to the prophet Jeremiah: "Even if Moses and Samuel
stood before Me, My soul would not be favorable toward them
[the Hebrews] … Who will spare you, O Jerusalem? Who will fear
for you?" (Jer 15:1, 5). This means that Moses and Samuel, though
already departed by the time of Jeremiah, can intercede for sinful
people. Judas Maccabeus saw a vision of the departed high priest,
Onias, who was "praying … for the whole nation of the Jews" and,
pointing to another man, who was with him, said to Judas: "This
is Jeremiah, the prophet of God, a man who loves his brothers and
prays fervently for the people and the holy city" (2 Macc 15:12,
14LXX). And the holy Apostle Peter clearly promised his disciples
that after his death he would remember them: "Moreover I will be
careful to ensure that you always have a reminder of these things
after my decease" (2 Pet 1:15).

In the Book of Revelation the visions of St John the Theologian demonstrate that saints do pray for us, and their prayers, like
smoke from a censer, rise before God, and He receives them with
favor. Thus, the Word of God clearly teaches us to call upon the
saints in our prayers, and affirms that they send up their prayers
to God for us; and that He, the most gracious, receives their

intercessions. Let us remember the story of the Feast of the Protection of the Most Holy Mother of God. The Christians of Constantinople diligently prayed in the St Mary of Blachernae church when the city was threatened with destruction. It was then that St Andrew, the fool for Christ, and his disciple Epiphanius, saw the heavenly Queen with a number of the righteous praying for the Christians before the throne of God. The prayers of the righteous were heard, for the Christians were miraculously delivered from their inevitable plight.

CHAPTER THREE

The Fate in the Future Life of Sinful People, Unrepentant of Their Sins

A completely different fate awaits sinners in the future life. After its trials at the toll houses mentioned earlier, the sinful soul is at the mercy of the demons' authority, and they drag it off into a place of "darkness and gloom," into hell, a fiery furnace. St John Chrysostom, when asked where was hell, this place of torture, said appropriately: "One asks exactly where is hell: but why should this be any person's business? One must know that it exists, and not where it is hidden…; therefore, we should continue our search not into where it is, but—how to avoid it."

What will be the life of sinners in hell? This will be a life amid torments. The torment of sinners will be caused by a clear recognition of their sins committed during their lives, and from pangs of conscience, which will awaken with full force and wrack the sinful soul, "Their worm does not die" (Mark 9:44). The soul will be alarmed by longing for earthly pleasures, now lost forever; aware too, that it is removed from communion with God and His saints, and must now dwell together with the other sinful souls, and the company of angry demons. It will be especially troubled by the thought that after the last judgment of Christ even greater sufferings await it.

However, it must be noted that the sufferings in hell will not be the same for all sinners, the degree of tortures will depend on the degree of their sinfulness. Just as there are many mansions in the heavenly Kingdom, so in hell there will be specific sections for various forms of punishment.

The tortures of hell inescapably await all unrepentant sinners. But glory and thanks to the mercy of the Lord! Glory and thanks to the power of the redemption of Christ our Saviour on the Cross! It reaches out to people even on the other side of the grave, until the general last judgment. Glory, too, for the infinite justice of God! Punishing sin and evil, it cannot leave virtue without reward, even if this virtue was only just begun.

The Orthodox Church confesses that the punishment of souls which before parting with the present life did repent, but were not able to bring forth worthy fruits of repentance, such as prayer, contrition for sins, fasting, alms, and, in general, deeds of Christian charity—the suffering of such souls is mixed with some consolation, and their state is not hopeless, for they are not completely lost from the kingdom of God. For them there still remains the possibility of receiving an easing of their sufferings: the chance to pass from a very grievous section of hell to one less so, and even to pass completely to blessedness. Jesus Christ Himself teaches us that forgiveness of sins is possible even after the death of a sinner (see Matt 12:32)—which means that leaving hell is possible. Of course, sinners themselves, by their own efforts or merits, can no longer ease their state, for after death there is no more activity or repentance—but their fate is altered by the prayers of the Church, and its children who remain on earth. They are also helped by charitable deeds, faithfully performed on earth in their remembrance, and especially by the power of the bloodless sacrifice [the

Eucharist] which is offered by the priest for each Christian and by the Catholic and Apostolic Church for all Christians in general.[2]

The holy Apostle John testifies that our prayers for the brethren, both living and departed, can grant them eternal life as long as they are not in mortal sin (see 1 John 5:16)—mortal sin being any sin the person did not repent of. Prayers for the dead are pleasing to God because we are asking for the salvation of a soul, a being dear to Him, created in the image and likeness of God and redeemed by the most pure blood of His Son; and too, the Lord says, "I do not will the death of the ungodly man. So the ungodly man should turn from his way and live" (Ezek 33:11).

Alms, distributed by the living in memory of the departed, by increasing the number of those praying (by virtue of their having received alms) for the salvation of the departed souls, are received by the Lord as if performed by the departed themselves. Many examples from the lives of the saints confirm this point.

Most helpful to the departed is the liturgy served in their memory. Is it possible that this great sacrament of the Only-begotten Son of God will not propitiate the righteous judgment of the most merciful God? Oh! With unwavering faith let us continue to believe that there shall be a mitigation of the fate beyond the grave for all our fathers, brothers, and sisters departed in the faith, through the power of the bloodless sacrifice. For this reason all types of liturgies, beginning with the apostolic ones, include prayers for the departed. The power of these prayers is confirmed by the holy Fathers. For example, St Cyril of Jerusalem says: "Souls, on behalf of which prayers are brought, will have the greatest benefit at the time of the offering of the holy and awesome Sacrifice," that is the body and blood of the Saviour. St John Chrysostom states: "Not lightly did the apostles establish the remembrance of the departed at the service of the awesome Gifts. They knew that this brought much help and benefit. For when the awesome Sacrifice is offered, how can we not pray to the merciful God for them?"

However, it is necessary to note, brethren, that our prayers and those of the Church are beneficial only for those who departed to the life beyond the grave with at least the beginnings of good: with faith in the Lord Jesus Christ, with hope in His mercy, and with repentance of sins. The most grievous sinners can receive mitigation of their fate, and even be completely relieved of hell's torture, but only if they died in repentance and faith. But woe to unconfessed sinners, freethinkers, blasphemers, and those stubborn in their unbelief. Their destiny is the eternal tortures of hell. They shall not be aided by the prayers of the Church, for in denying faith in Christ, denying their sins, and spurning the prayers of the Church, they blaspheme the Holy Spirit which is active in the Church. Blasphemy of the Holy Spirit, according to the words of Christ, "will not be forgiven him, either in this age or in the age to come" (Matt 12:32). Prayers for such sinners do not help them, but benefit only the supplicators themselves according to the Prophet David: "and my prayer shall turn into mine own bosom" (Ps 34:13 LXX).

In the teachings of the Orthodox Church presented, one can see that the departed are either in paradise, or in hell, in torments.

There is no middle stage between paradise and hell; such a stage is recognized only by Roman Catholics. According to their teaching, the souls of people who depart in penitence, but lack its fruits, are to be found in the fires of purgatory, and suffer there for a time, until by their own sufferings they atone for all of their sins. But this teaching is not Orthodox. The Lord and Saviour in His parable on the rich man and Lazarus did not point out any middle state between *Abraham's bosom* and *hell*, which means there is no such state. What other new sufferings are necessary in the propitiation of God's justice when the blood of Jesus Christ redeems us from all sins? If a person, while living on earth, repudiated faith in Christ, can he possibly be reconciled to God by his tortures in the fire of purgatory?

This, Orthodox Christians, is the teaching of the Church concerning the life of the departed until the general great judgment. This teaching does not give the answers to questions of a mind that is idly curious, but it does present many edifying lessons for us. From it we learn that there is a most intimate bond between our present life and the life hereafter. Our present life is a beginning, and the hereafter is the continuation and result of it; the first is *sowing*, and the second the *harvest*. What you sow here, that you will harvest there. For this reason it is necessary for us to try to have a good beginning, an abundantly good sowing, a sowing not for the *body*, but for the *soul*, as is said by the Apostle Paul: "For he who sows to his flesh will of the flesh reap corruption, but he who sows to the Spirit will of the Spirit reap everlasting life" (Gal 6:8).

Secondly, we find that the soul after separating from this world, passes into another world—the spiritual realm. Therefore, it is necessary to become acquainted with that world in advance, in order to nurture in oneself beforehand a love for everything heavenly and godly. Thirdly, we discover that after our death, our soul immediately awaits a just and impartial trial, followed by the reward for the deeds of our life. For this reason, it is necessary for us to make a reckoning of our debts here, by confessing our sins, cleansing our soul, and doing deeds of love for God and our neighbor; so that, having accomplished the course of life, we should not fall into the hands of angry demons, but be found worthy to be carried up by angelic hands into Abraham's bosom.

Most importantly is to pray to our Lord and Saviour that He would help us, through the prayers of the most pure Mother of God, all the righteous of God, and the intercession of our guardian angel, to attain the blessedness of paradise and to be in communion with the saints who have pleased God. It behooves us brethren to remember these thoughts more often for much good will come of it. Remember the end—your death—as it teaches the Word of God, and you will never sin (see Sir 7:36 LXX).

Blessed are those of us, who in the troubles and sorrows of the present life search for consolation in God and with diligence pray to the saints, for that prayer will not be in vain. Each of us has had occasion to be convinced of this thought. That is why all saints revered by us are called intercessors, for they defend us in trouble, assist us in bodily suffering, comfort the sorrowing and the angry, and plead for sinners who have sincerely repented.

We should add that the saintly righteous are always prepared to pray for us since they themselves once lived on earth, suffered afflictions, and know by personal experience, how difficult it is for man to struggle with worldly calamities and grief, and know how necessary in the battle is heavenly assistance.

The saints love us spiritually, for they, descending from the same ancestors as we, are related to us, and are our brothers in the faith. Though they reside in heaven now, they always remember their earthly homeland and are ever ready to intercede before God on behalf of His people. If we, who are sinful, assist our neighbors, then all the more so do the saints who cannot remain disinterested observers of our troubles. With a love more complete and pure than ours, they cannot help but pray and intercede before God for us. How consoling all of this is to us sinners! This love of the saints should urge us to call upon them more frequently and more zealously for they are our "speedy helpers and intercessors."[3] For these reasons every church service ends with this appeal to Jesus Christ, that He save and have mercy on us, through the "prayers of His most pure Mother and all the saints."[4]

Chapter Four

The Incorruptibility and Miraculous Powers of Holy Relics

The Incorrupt Hand of St John Chrysostom

We stated earlier that the Lord glorifies saints through the incorruptibility of their relics. While the bodies of the deceased are generally subject to corruption, the bodies of some saints, by the will of God, remain incorruptible on earth for many years. This incorruption is a visible witness of the holiness of the saints, and a visible sign of God's blessing residing in their very bodies. In them the words of David have come true, not only in relation to the Saviour but to his faithful servants as well: "Because Thou shalt not leave my soul in hell, neither shalt Thou suffer Thine Holy One to see corruption" (Ps 15:10 LXX). The incorruptibility of relics is beyond all doubt. Those Whom the Lord has vouchsafed to see the incorrupt relics of His saints and to venerate them with faith will witness to their incorruptibility before the whole world. In Kiev, Novgorod, Moscow, Voronezh, and Zadonsk the incorrupt relics of saints were openly at rest and by their miracles witnessed to the power of God residing in them. How many relics of saints are still hidden? The relics of Saints Zosima and Sabbatius of Solovetsky Monastery, Sergius and Herman of Valaam, Arsenius of Komel, Alexander Nevsky, and the newly canonized righteous ones, St John of Kronstadt, the elders of Optina, Ambrose and Nectarios, and others still hidden, pour forth numerous blessings on us![5]

Many holy Fathers write of the incorruption and miraculous powers of relics. St Ephraim the Syrian says: "Even after death, saints act as they did when living, healing the sick, expelling demons, and by the power of the Lord repelling every evil action of their torturous realm. For the miracle-working blessing of the Holy Spirit is always inherent in holy relics." With these words St John Chrysostom invited all to approach the relics of St Ignatius the God-bearer: "If you are sorrowful, ill, wronged, in some other trouble, or in the depths of sin, run to him with faith: you will receive aid and depart with great happiness, sensing an easing of your conscience … This treasure is needful for all: for the unfortunate, since it frees them from calamities, and for the fortunate, for it confirms their fortune, and for the ailing, for it returns well-being to them, and for the healthy, for it turns away disease."[6]

We revere not only the incorruptible bodies of saints, but also the instruments of the suffering and death of the martyrs, and the belongings which were used by the saints during their lives. Such relics through which we receive blessings include the robe and belt of the Mother of God, the chains of the Apostle Peter, and the handkerchiefs and towels of the Apostle Paul that performed miracles.[7]

CHAPTER FIVE

The Veneration of Holy Icons

F inally, we also honor icons of the saints. Looking at the image of the saint, we carry our thoughts from the icon to the saint himself; from the image we are transferred to the person. Revering icons, we revere not the wood or paints, not the gold or silver decorating the icon, but those persons which are represented on the icon. But one might ask, why bow to icons, when we can mentally raise our thoughts to the saints themselves? This is easy to explain from the bond which exists between our soul and body. Our soul, closely united to the body, cannot have a pure and clear understanding of things unseen; for this it needs visible images. For this reason, God Himself appeared to the Old Testament righteous people in the form of a man, and instructed Moses to place golden representations of cherubim in the altar; such representations were also in the temple of Solomon.

The necessity of icons is also confirmed in the New Testament. We know that the Lord sent His own image Not-Made-by-Hands to Abgar, ruler of Edessa,[8] and that St Luke painted images of the Mother of God. During times of persecution, Christians carried icons to the caves and there offered heartfelt prayer before them. In accordance with this early Christian example we place icons in prominent places of our churches and homes, light lamps before them, and burning incense, we bow before them and kiss them. The veneration of icons is logical; those whom we love and respect, we desire to see as often as possible, in this way showing them respect. We collect their portraits and decorate our homes with pictures of our father, mother, brother, husband, wife, and others in order to transfer to those pictures the love and respect which we feel for the prototypes. How is it possible then for us not to venerate the icons of the Lord, the Mother of God, and the righteous? St Basil the Great writes: "I accept the holy apostles, prophets, and martyrs, and invoke their intercession before God ... I also revere the drawings of their icons and bow before them, especially for the reason that they came down from the time of the holy apostles ... and are pictured in all our churches." The Seventh Ecumenical Council called the veneration of holy icons "a tradition of the Catholic Church which accepted the Gospel from all the ends of the earth."

The most powerful witness to the holiness of icons is the innumerable signs and miracles which the Lord condescends to accomplish through icons, especially those termed *miraculous*. Orthodox Russia abounded with such icons, and several have been brought overseas. Brethren, have recourse to these fountains of healing and be cured of your illnesses:

some from despondency,
some from passions,
some from life's sorrows,
some from bodily illnesses,
but all from wounds of the soul—our sins!

Let us remind ourselves now brethren of everything we have said about glorifying the righteous. In heaven they are unutterably blissful, awaiting yet greater bliss in the future. We on earth call on them in prayer and venerate their icons and incorruptible relics through which the Lord grants us sinners abundant miraculous assistance. How consoling it is to think that even among us there are imitators of the saintly righteous ones, and that from among us some will be found who will be vouchsafed the same glory of the saints in heaven and the same honor on earth.

❖ Chapter Six
Christ's Holy Church

So that people might attain eternal salvation for themselves, the Lord founded the Church, His grace-filled kingdom on earth, imparting grace to all members of the Church—power which sanctifies them. He established sacraments for the Church as the means by which we receive this grace-filled power.

The name of the Church of Christ is used in two ways, either in a general sense or in a more inclusive manner. In a general sense the Church is a society of all free, intelligent beings, of both angels and people, believing in Christ the Saviour and united in Him as its one head. The holy Apostle Paul understands the Church in this way when He says that God ordained the union of all things in heaven and earth under Christ the Head and placed Him as the Head of the Church (see Eph 1:10, 23; Col 1:18), to which therefore people and angels belong. For angels too believe in Christ as the true God-man and serve as His ministers in establishing the Church on earth; they are sent by Him to assist every man in inheriting salvation (see Heb 1:14). In a narrower sense the Church of Christ is composed strictly of people professing the faith of Christ, whether they live on earth, or have already passed into the future life. Those living on earth compose the kingdom of grace, the earthly or militant Church, while the departed compose the kingdom of glory, the heavenly, triumphant Church.

But why must believers in Christ be saved not as individuals, but together? Why must they belong not only to an internal, spiritual union, but also to an external, visible union? Firstly, this relationship provides a healthy understanding of the Church, and secondly it is the way established by God Himself.

A similar pattern of organization is found in daily life. People of one descent aspire to the same aim, and form not only an internal, spiritual union, but also an external and visible union. They arrange general conferences, the strong cooperate with the weak, and the experienced with the less expert. In this way the family circle is formed, as are the circle of relatives and as is the circle or society of citizens. Through such union, societies become stronger, develop, and consolidate their existence for longer periods of time. Does it not follow from this that people who believe in the One True God, confessing the One Christ, Son of God, incarnate as man, redeemed by His most pure Blood, sanctified by the grace of the One Holy Spirit, must belong to an intimate union; not only internal, but also an external, visible one?

If we shall preserve not only unity in faith with all the children of Christ's Church, but will also be united as members of the Church visibly—participate in church gatherings and fulfill all her rules—then the Church will be as close to us as our own mother. In her we shall find for ourselves a sinless teacher of faith and piety, a supplicator for us in the present and future life, a comforter amid life's sorrows, and a trustworthy guide to the heavenly fatherland. But, if while preserving in our soul the true faith, and regarding ourselves children of Christ's Church, we shall begin to alienate ourselves from the Church—shall discontinue our attendance at prayerful gatherings, shall not be fervent fulfillers of pious rituals, shall gradually begin to lose the habit of Church attendance—then our ties to the Church will begin to weaken and eventually be cut. We shall find ourselves alone amid life's waves and then the destruction of our souls will be assured.

Orthodox Christians, this is how necessary it is that people who espouse faith in Christ be truly children of the Church of Christ. In the instructions of the Word of God, we find even more solid reasons for not withdrawing from the Church. The Word of God teaches us that God Himself founded the Church, gathered His children together, and returned to the enclosure of salvation those who were torn from it by enemy forces.

We know that the first Church of our sinless ancestors was in paradise, and who founded it? It was formed by God Himself Who created Adam and Eve in His own image, having given them the commandment to consecrate the seventh day to God. When the first people sinned, and the Church of the sinless was destroyed, the Lord, having given people the promise of the Saviour, reestablished the Church, not of the sinless, but of those to be saved. During the long period of the Old Testament, this Church of salvation was exposed many times to the danger of destruction from the devil's snares and from the enemies of the Church, both seen and unseen. The Hebrew people, chosen by God, often fell into sin and idol worship. During these dark years of decline in the Church, the laws of Moses were broken, the temple fell into neglect, idols replaced the sacrificial altar, and sacrifices to Baal, Moloch, and other idols were brought openly to Jerusalem. But the Lord restored the failing Church, raised up prophets and pious kings, and by the miraculous action of His providence returned apostates to the way of truth. The temple was cleansed of pagan abominations and people again gathered to hear and learn the law of the Lord. Thus the Lord shepherded the Old Testament Church up to the coming into the world of the Saviour, Who was to restore David's fallen tabernacle and gather the believers into one flock, "as a hen gathers her chicks under her wings" (Matt 23:37). He "gather[ed] together in one the children of God who were scattered abroad" (John 11:52) and built the New Testament Church, which could not be defeated by the gates of hell, and which would continue until the end of the age.

How did the Lord form this Christian Church? From the many people who accepted His teaching, He selected twelve at first, and then seventy disciples, and appointed them as teachers for all believers. At first He sent them to preach only to the lost sheep of the house of Israel, and then to the whole world, to preach the Gospel to all people. In order to strengthen the Church, the Lord established seven sacraments and prompted His followers to obey the people chosen by Him, as they would obey God Himself; finally, having brought Himself as a sacrifice for all mankind, the Lord called all to partake of the blessings of the heavenly Kingdom, and sent down on them the Holy Spirit. The apostles, cloaked in power from above, "went out and preached everywhere, the Lord working with them and confirming the word through the accompanying signs" (Mark 16:20). Finding believers in the teaching of Christ they formed societies in cities, calling them Churches; they inspired members of the Church to preserve the unity of faith in an alliance of peace, teaching them to be members of one body, to keep one faith and one spirit, to accept communion from one bread, and not to withdraw from general gatherings, for to do so risked the danger of separation from the Church and eternal ruin. It was in this manner that the one Church of Christ, embracing all believers in Christ, was begun and confirmed.

Since the Founder of the Church, the Lord Jesus Christ, wants all people to be saved and come to the knowledge of the truth, then all people must be members of the Church, all the descendants of Adam, who together with him sinned and were guilty. But in reality, not all people are members of the Church, only those who through the portal of baptism enter the saving fold of the Church. It follows then that neither the Jews, nor the Muslims, nor pagans, not yet having received the good news or baptism in Christ, belong to the Church; not belonging to the Church are also those who, though having received the good news of Christ and entered the ranks of the catechumens, have not as yet been deemed worthy of holy baptism. In order to truly become members of the Church, according to St John Chrysostom, they must "enter within, pass through the courtyard, see Holiness, penetrate into the Holy of Holies, and be with the Trinity."

But even among those who have already entered the Church through the door of baptism, not all consistently reserve for themselves the holy right to be members of the Church. For salvation, it is necessary not only to enter the Church, but to continue to be a true and obedient repository of the holy teaching of the Church, to continually feel in one's self a filial sense toward the Church, to always acknowledge the debt of seeing in the Church one's spiritual mother, who has regenerated us in holy baptism. An epistle of the Eastern Patriarchs refers to this point: "We believe that members of the Universal Church are only the faithful who undoubtedly confess the pure faith of Jesus Christ, which we accepted from Christ Himself, from the apostles and the holy ecumenical councils, even though some of them may be subject to various sins. For, if the faithful who have sinned were not members of the Church, they would not be subject to its judgment.

But she does judge them, calls them to repentance, and leads them in the path of salutary commandments; and therefore, in spite of their being exposed to sin, they remain and are acknowledged as members of the Universal Church as long as they do not apostatize, but adhere to the universal Orthodox faith."

It is affirmed that only in the Church of Christ is it possible to acquire salvation and eternal life, that outside the Church there is no salvation, and from this we receive the lesson to always remain members of the Church. Only under this condition is it possible to preserve the faith in all its purity; only in the Church can one receive sanctifying powers leading to life and piety; only in her is a truly pious life possible. This lesson was continually reiterated by the holy Fathers of the Church when exhorting apostates and dissenters. St Irenaeus, an apostolic father, writes: "Where the Church is, there also is the Spirit of God; where the Spirit of God is, there is the Church and the fullness of grace: for the Spirit is the truth. That is why those who are not partakers of Him, do not feed at the mother's breast to receive life, and do not find for themselves in the Body of Jesus Christ a copious fountain, but dig in the earth wells of destruction for themselves, and drink from pools of foul water, withdrawing from the faith of the Church, rejecting the Spirit, in order not to be enlightened by Him." The same truth is expressed by St Cyprian, bishop of Carthage, a Church Father of the third century: "He who has not the Church for a mother cannot have God for his father. If anyone who was outside of Noah's ark could be saved, then those found outside the Church could also be saved." In order to instruct us, the Lord says: "He who is not with Me is against Me, and he who does not gather with Me scatters abroad" (Matt 12:30). As the blessed Augustine teaches: "Everyone who has severed himself from communion with the

Church, even though his life be worthy of praise, only for that one iniquity of leaving union with Christ, will not have life, but the anger of God will reside on him."

Orthodox Catechism teaches us that even though Jesus Christ truly gave Himself as a sacrifice for all, and brought grace and salvation to all, only those of us will profit by this who in turn voluntarily accept participation in His sufferings, in conformity with His death. In order for the Lord to truly be our Saviour, we must be cleansed of sins, changed from sinners into saints, and be liberated from all destructive consequences of sin, temporary and everlasting. Without fulfilling these conditions, we not only shall not attain that bliss which Christ prepared for us, but on the contrary, we shall find eternal destruction here. Eternal grief will befall us, the present children of the Church, if we, hearing the teaching of Christ, shall not adopt it with all the powers of our souls, shall reject the grace-filled powers granted to us, which are for our life and piety, and by our sins and unbelief smother within ourselves the voice of the Spirit Who instructs us in every truth. But the Lord, not desiring the death of a sinner, gives to each one of us ways of assimilating those blessings which He has prepared for those to be saved. He sanctifies us and helps us to "put on the new man which was created according to God, in true righteousness and holiness" (Eph 4:24). When the end of life comes for every man, and the end of the earthly existence of the whole of mankind, then the Lord will bring all to trial and will "reward each according to his works" (Matt 16:27).

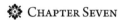

CHAPTER SEVEN

The Characteristics of People before the End of the World. A Prophecy

The particular judgment of the departed will occur immediately after their death, but the general (last) judgment will take place at the second coming of Christ; to determine exactly when this time will come is impossible, for this is hidden not only from people, but even from the angels. "But of that day and hour no one knows, not even the angels of heaven, but My Father only" (Matt 24:36), said our Divine Teacher to His disciples, when they asked Him about this matter. It is hidden from us too, in order that we be ready at any moment, with a clear conscience to appear before the judgment seat of the impartial Judge, so that we do not give ourselves to carelessness about our salvation, but, like the wise virgins, will be ready to meet the Heavenly Bridegroom worthily and to enter the bridal chamber with Him. This is why Jesus Christ often encouraged His disciples to keep vigil, so that the coming of the Son of Man would not catch them unawares: "Watch therefore, for you do not know what hour your Lord is coming... you also be ready, for the Son of Man is coming at an hour you do not expect" (Matt 24:42, 44). "Take heed, watch and pray; for you do not know when the time is [the second coming]. . . . and what I say to you, I say to all: Watch!" (Mark 13:33, 37). If for our own good—through God's providence—the day and hour of the second coming of Christ is hidden from us, then the same Lord, "who desires all men to be saved" (1 Tim 2:4), and desires for the strengthening of the righteous and for the instruction of sinners, He deigned to reveal signs to us by which we can judge the time of His second coming.

The first of these signs is the universal awareness of Christ's gospel. The message about Christ will be spread to all nations of the world; not one nation, or tribe, even in the farthest and unknown corners of the earth, will be left without the enlightenment of Christ's teaching. The last commandment of Jesus Christ will be fulfilled—"Go into all the world and preach the gospel to every creature" (Mark 16:15), and "Go therefore and make disciples of all the nations" (Matt 28:19). Another sign of the approach of the second coming of Christ will be the great impoverishment of faith and love among people. The primordial enemy (the devil), sowing the weeds of falsehood and delusion amid the good seed of God's Word before the end of the world, will direct all his powers and means in order if possible to unconditionally tear away from the kingdom of God all those who are called to it or have already entered it, and to subjugate them to his destructive dominion. Jesus Christ taught His disciples, "Then if anyone says to you, 'Look, here is the Christ!' or 'There!' do not believe it. For false christs and false prophets will rise and show great signs and wonders to deceive, if possible, even the elect. See, I have told you beforehand. Therefore if they say to you, 'Look, He is in the desert!' do not go out; or 'Look, He is in the inner rooms!' do not believe it" (Matt 24:23–26, compare with Mark 13:21–23). The result of this will be that many will be seduced and many will be deceived (see Matt 24:10). "And because lawlessness will abound, the love of many will grow cold" (Matt 24:12), and there shall follow "'the abomination of desolation,' spoken of by Daniel the prophet, standing in the holy place" (Matt 24:15); "when the Son of Man comes, will He really find faith on the earth?" (Luke 18:8).

In the First Epistle to Timothy, the Apostle Paul writes: "Now the Spirit expressly says that in latter times some will depart from the faith, giving heed to deceiving spirits and doctrines of demons" (1 Tim 4:1). In his Second Epistle to Timothy, he offers a gloomy portrait of mankind's religious and moral condition: "in the last days perilous times will come: For men will be lovers of themselves, lovers of money, boasters, proud, blasphemers, dis-obedient to parents, unthankful, unholy, unloving, unforgiving, slanderers, without self-control, brutal, despisers of good, traitors, headstrong, haughty, lovers of pleasure rather than lovers of God, having a form of godliness but denying its power" (2 Tim 3:1–5).

The holy Apostle Jude witnesses to the agreement of all the apostles on this point: "remember the words which were spoken before by the apostles of our Lord Jesus Christ: how they told you that there would be mockers in the last time who would walk according to their own ungodly lusts. These are sensual persons, who cause divisions, not having the Spirit" (Jude 17–19). The Lord Himself foretold that at the end of the world "many false proph-ets will rise up and deceive many. And because lawlessness will abound, the love of many will grow cold" (Matt 24:11, 12), so that "when the Son of Man comes, will He really find faith on the earth?" (Luke 18:8).

Such a decline in faith and love among people will result first in the appearance of many false prophets and horrible internecine wars, and secondly, great and serious calamities in the physical world. The gospel will be known to all, but some will not believe it; a greater number will hold heretical opinions, following not the God-given teaching, but building up their own religion, of their own fabrication, though based on the words of Scripture. These self-fabricated faiths will be numerous. Their roots are found in the papacy, and then continued by Luther and Calvin. The latter two, by setting as a principle their own personal understanding of faith from Scripture only, gave a strong impetus toward the invention of various confessions. Although there are many now, there will be more. For every kingdom their own faith, and later for every province, and then for every city, and finally, perhaps, for every person, his own faith. Wherever people devise their religions for themselves, it cannot be otherwise. And all such faiths will continue to appropriate to themselves the name of Christian.

There will be some who do maintain the true faith, as given by the holy Apostles and kept in the Orthodox Church; but even among these, many will be Orthodox in name only. They will not have in their hearts that order which is demanded by the faith, for they will be entranced by the present age. This is how broad the future field of apostasy will be! Even though the name "Christian" will be heard everywhere, and churches and rites will be widespread, all of this will only be outward; internally there will be complete apostasy.

The Antichrist will be born under such conditions, and will be reared in that spirit of pretense which is opposed to reality. Giving himself wholly to Satan, he will openly apostasize, and armed with his captivating intrigues, he will draw into apostasy, from Christ the Lord, all those not holding the Christian faith in truth, forcing them to worship him as god. The elect of God will not be deceived, though he will attempt to entice them too. To save His elect the Lord will end those evil days. The Lord will appear and destroy the Antichrist and all his works by His coming.[9]

CHAPTER EIGHT

Apostasy in the Last Days of the World

The apostasy of New Israel (the Christians) from the Saviour at the end of time will be an extensive phenomenon, as the Apostle foretold: "the falling away comes first," and later, as a result and fruit of falling away, "the man of sin is revealed, the son of perdition" (2 Thess 2:2–3); he will dare to call himself the promised Messiah, will demand godly worship for himself, and will receive it from those who have prepared themselves to receive the Antichrist by either openly or secretly falling away from Christ. Apostasy will be so widespread that "because lawlessness will abound, the love of many will grow cold" (Matt 24:12). This means that sinful temptations and behavior will increase so much that they will entice many people into sinful lives. Faith in Christ will barely exist, as the Lord Himself declared: "when the Son of Man comes, will He really find faith on the earth?" (Luke 18:8).

Temporary, material pursuits and pleasures will completely attract the attention of mankind. "And as it was in the days of Noah," says the Gospel, "so it will be also in the days of the Son of Man: They ate, they drank, they married wives, they were given in marriage, until the day that Noah entered the ark, and the flood came and destroyed them all. Likewise as it was also in the days of Lot: They ate, they drank, they bought, they sold, they planted, they built" (Luke 17:26–28).

Bountiful worldly progress and huge earthly enterprises, visible to all are described by the Word of God as a sign of the last days and the fruition of mankind's sinfulness. This state, for the most part, will not be obvious to mankind at first glance. Mankind never will admit itself to be a disciple of evil, even though it be drowning in evil; it continually aspires to express itself as virtuous. Attachment to materialism and to material success can easily seize the whole person, seize his mind, his heart, and capture all of his time and strength: As a result of my fall, "My soul cleaveth to the dust" (Ps 118:25 LXX) instead of abiding above. This attachment distracts man from the Word of God and thoughts of death and eternity, and diverts him from faith and the knowledge of God, and destroys him with eternal death.

The Holy Spirit of God announces to everyone without exception: "If anyone loves the world" (i.e., earthly life with its successes and pleasures), "the love of [God] the Father is not in him" (1 John 2:15). "Do you not know that friendship with the world is enmity with God? Whoever therefore wants to be a friend of the world makes himself an enemy of God" (Jas 4:4). "You cannot serve God and mammon" (Matt 6:24). Serving mammon (the god of money or earthly gain), especially when all the powers of the soul are sacrificed to this service, is a falling away from the serving of God, and is a sure sign of falling into the deepest abyss of sinfulness with no way out.

As ancient Israel sacrificed the spiritual dignity offered it by the Redeemer for earthly advantages and futile hopes of super-abundant earthly success, so the New Israel (the Christians), as witnessed by Holy Scripture, will reject its spiritual dignity, already granted by the Redeemer, for the sake of fleeting material success.

Ancient Israel was deceived by dreams of earthly successes and the New Israel will be fooled by similar dreams and aspirations. For their rejection of the Redeemer, ancient Israel was overtaken by temporary and eternal calamities. These disasters are only a feeble prefiguration of the horrible catastrophes which will be the punishment for New Israel for its transgressions. It will be subject to fierce punishment, both temporal and eternal, which it will not escape if it neglects "so great a salvation, which at first began to be spoken by the Lord, and was confirmed to us by those who heard Him, God also bearing witness both with signs and wonders, with various miracles, and gifts of the Holy Spirit, according to His own will" (Heb 2:3–4).

At this point the question will be raised, what must we do in order not to fall away from the Redeemer and not to incur the anger of God? The Apostle Paul answers: "Therefore we must give the more earnest heed to the things we have heard, lest we drift away" (Heb 2:1). This means that we must devote special attention to the New Testament, in which God has deigned to join with us, uniting us with Himself by the holy sacraments, revealing to us His most holy and perfect will in the Gospel, crowning true children of the New Testament with the manifest and tangible gift of the Holy Spirit.

We need to remember the death and God's judgment to which we shall be subjected immediately after our separation from the body, and call to mind the blessed, or distressful, eternity which will be our destiny according to the pronouncement of God's judgment. In constant remembrance of death, God's judgment—and blessed eternity, the attitude of the heart toward earthly life—changes. A person begins to regard himself as a wanderer on earth, and a sense of coolness and indifference toward earthly objects appears in the heart. All attention is turned toward learning and fulfilling the gospel commandments.

As a traveler, having become lost in a thick forest on a dark night, tries to find his way home by the sound of a bell or a horn, so a true Christian, heeding the teaching of Christ, exerts himself to be free of the domain of his carnal mind, born and nourished by earthly life.

The majority of people, drunk on the false, seductive teachings of fallen spirits and violently agitated by the action of this teaching within themselves, have scorned the Word of God, and do not want to know It. But attention to this Word is most vital, so that we should never fall away! The events in today's world, which are so hostile to the words of the Gospel, justify the significance of struggling to follow precepts of the Word. This attentiveness is necessary if we are not to be irrevocably deprived of salvation. In His patient long-suffering and mercy Our Lord has not yet deprived mankind of the means for salvation, offering an opportunity to the diminishing remnant of those still believing in Him.[10]

When the Gospel reaches all peoples living on earth, and attracts all those capable of accepting its message and capable of being reborn through the grace of the Holy Spirit, then there will be no more reason for the present order to continue. The end of the world will come and the Lord will appear to pass judgment over those living on earth, leading some into the kingdom of His glory, and sending others to the bitter fate they have chosen for themselves.

In such a manner—either at the same time or after all of God's people come forth from out of humanity and there is nothing else left to expect—those who are then not of God, having thrown away their mask, will come forth and the harvest will be ready. The

Lord will send harvesters and the end will come. In the same way that the period of ripening before the harvest has its limit, so also these final events have their limit, determined by God. The good and the evil, already sown, will grow and develop, and they will ripen in their own time. This cannot take place before the allotted time. If one should ask the question, why are the harvesters not now coming to the field, the answer is simply that the time has not yet come, the harvest is not ready. To the question as to why those awaited world events are not yet visible to us, the answer is that the time for their appearance, by God's will, has not yet arrived. It is in this same context that the appearance of Antichrist belongs.

God has deemed to reveal to us a few of His plans for the world. Applying them to our topic we may be able to discern that which withholds the Antichrist (see 2 Thess 2:6). The world continues so that the power of salvation deposited by God into mankind will produce its result. The power of salvation is the Word of God and grace, accepted in faith, and put into practice by self-denying zeal for pleasing God. The Word of God walks the earth, stimulating the slumbering, and leading them to the fountains of grace. Re-born, they work out their own salvation, to the glory of God, who established salvation for all.

This activity takes place everywhere, among unbelievers, the lost, and true believers. Not all the called are the chosen, not all the fish in the net are fit for the table. Only those born from above, "not of blood, nor of the will of the flesh, nor of the will of man, but of God," are given "the right to become children of God" (John 1:12–13). With these the Lord builds His heavenly kingdom. The children of God are the material on earth prepared for heaven by the Word of God and grace, received by their own free will. When the Word of God and grace choose from the earth all the worthy material (for heaven), and the kingdom of God is completely built up, then the task of the salvation of the Lord will be complete and nothing will remain of the present order of things.

The world continues because not all who are suitable for the kingdom of Christ have entered it, or, not as many as are necessary have yet entered. The Lord has said: "And other sheep I have which are not of this fold; them also I must bring, and they will hear My voice; and there will be one flock and one shepherd" (John 10:16). When all seeking salvation in the true God have done so, then the end will draw near and the Antichrist will appear. Therefore, the reason for restraining his appearance will be that the power of salvation has not yet fully completed its work, and its continuing action restrains him. When this action has halted, then he will appear on the scene.

And what are the means for restraining the Antichrist so that the elect may be brought to salvation? Our fathers considered the withholding power of the Antichrist to be the Roman Empire. In their time the Roman Empire still existed and it was possible to support this interpretation based on the prophecy of the Prophet Daniel. In our times the only significance we can give to such an idea is within the context of understanding the Roman Empire to mean imperial (monarchial) power in general. Concerning such power, we should understand it to be a monarchy which has the ability to control social movement, and at the same time adhere to Christian principles. It does not allow the people to stray from these principles; it contains the people. Since the Antichrist will have as his main task the goal of attracting the people away from Christ, he therefore will not arrive if monarchy is still in control. This power will not allow him to appear; it impedes his negating spiritual activity. This is the withholding power. When the monarchy falls, and everywhere nations institute self-government (republics, democracies), then the Antichrist will be able to act freely. It will not be difficult for Satan to prepare voters to renounce Christ as experience taught us during the French Revolution. There will be no one to veto the movement. A humble declaration of faith will not be heard. Thus, when such a social order is instituted everywhere, making it easy for antichristian movements to appear, then the Antichrist will come forth. Up until that time he will wait; he is impeded. It is St John Chrysostom's words that lead us to this thought of a time when monarchy was understood to mean the Roman Empire: "When it is said that the Roman government has ceased to be, then the Antichrist will appear. Until that time the government (monarchy) will be feared. No one will easily follow the Antichrist. After this time, when such control will be liquidated, anarchy will triumph, and the Antichrist will try to capture all human and divine power."

It would be easy to assume that the people might be able to preserve their faith. But as was mentioned before, it is difficult to imagine that in the course of time faith might grow in strength. The bright, hopeful picture painted by some authors of Christian works of a good future would be pleasant to encounter, though there is no basis to justify such a hope. The grace-filled kingdom of Christ indeed is increasing, growing, filling up, not visibly on the earth but rather in the heavens, invisibly. It is made up of people, here and there in the earthly kingdoms who have been prepared for that place by the salvific power of Christ. On earth, the reign of disbelief and evil are predictable. It visibly expands and when it already is very much advanced, then the process will only have begun. It will take only one influential example or strong voice, and apostasy from faith will have begun. This jolt will be given by the Antichrist.[11]

St Cyril of Jerusalem in his catechetical teaching on the Antichrist says: "We search for our own sign in regard to the coming of Christ; but belonging to the Church, we should look for a church sign. The Saviour says: 'And then many will offended, will betray one another, and will hate one another'" (Matt 24:10). If you hear that bishops attack bishops even unto bloodletting, clergy against clergy, and laymen against laymen, do not be bewildered for this is foretold in the Scriptures; do not look at what happens today, but at what is written. Even though I, who teach you, perish, you shall not perish together with me; it is possible for a disciple to be better than the teacher, and be first among the latecomers; since the Master also receives those who come at the eleventh hour. If betrayal appeared even among the apostles, why should we wonder, if brotherly hatred will appear among bishops? But the signs refer not only to the rulers of the Church, but also to laymen. For Christ says that because of the spread of iniquity, the love of many shall wax cold. Shall any of those present be able to boast that he has an unhypocritical love for his neighbor? In most cases is it not rather that people kiss others, show a joyful appearance and happy glance, but in their hearts prepare snares, "speak peace to their neighbors, but imagine mischief in their hearts." (Ps 27:3 LXX)?

Hate among brothers is already an invitation for Antichrist. For the devil first promotes discord among people, in order that when the Antichrist comes, they would more easily accept him. God forbid that any one of those serving Christ anywhere should unite with this enemy!

Formerly there were open heretics, but now the Church is filled with secret heretics. People have strayed from the truth "they will not endure sound doctrine ... because they have itching ears" (2 Tim 4:3). Say a flattering word to build up their self-esteem and all listen in satisfaction. Appeal to them to change, and all turn away. The majority have retreated from correct understanding, and more conveniently choose evil, rather than accepting the good. And this is the apostasy, after which the enemy can be expected. He has already begun to send his forerunners, in order that the way be prepared for his hunt. For that reason, beware brother, and strengthen your soul.

The Church witnesses today before the Living God, warns against Antichrist in advance of his coming. Whether this occurs during your life, we do not know; whether this happens after, we do not know. In the meantime, it would be well, if, knowing this, you would be forewarned.

The true Christ, the Only-begotten Son of God, will not again come from this world. If anyone claiming false visions appears in the desert, do not go out. If they say, "'Look, here is the Christ!' or, 'Look, He is there!'" (Mark 13:21), do not believe it. Do not look down to the earth anymore; for the Master will descend from heaven, not alone, as before, but escorted by many myriads of angels; not secretly, as rain in the dark, but He will openly shine like lightning. For He Himself said: "For as the lightning comes from the east and flashes to the west, so also will the coming of the Son of Man be" (Matt 24:27).

Just as before His Incarnation, when it was expected that God would be born of the Virgin, Satan, with evil intent, perverted this truth by means of a fabled teaching among idol worshipers that false gods give birth and are born of women, in order that when this lie was received, people would believe it, instead of the truth. In like manner before the second coming of the true Christ, the adversary, having turned to his own benefit the expectation of ordinary people, will produce a certain sorcerer, very experienced in the deceptive and evil art of magic and sorcery, who will usurp all power to himself, falsely proclaiming himself as Christ, and under the name of Christ shall beguile the Jews in their expectation of the Messiah, and shall deceive pagans (and apostates from Christianity) by sorcery.

The foretold Antichrist will come only after the coming of worldwide anarchy and the struggle of various parties. When the end of the world draws near, ten rulers shall arise in various places, all ruling at the same time. The Antichrist will be the eleventh, and will usurp all rule by the skillful use of evil sorcery. He will overthrow three of those who became rulers before him, having in his own power the remaining seven. At first, he will display the good sense and love for man befitting a person of wisdom and renown; having seduced the Jews, as if he were the expected Christ, by signs, miracles, and fraudulent, flattering sorcery. Later, he will become known for all kinds of evil, inhuman, and lawless deeds. He will surpass all iniquitous and dishonorable men who had lived before him, harboring destructive, brutal, and unkind thoughts against all, especially against Christians. He will act in these ways for three years and six months and will be stopped only by the second glorious coming from heaven of the Only-begotten Son of God, our Lord and Saviour, Jesus Christ. The Lord will destroy Antichrist by the "breath of His mouth" (2 Thess 2:8) and consign him to the flames of hell.[12]

CHAPTER NINE

Signs by Which the Nearness of the Second Coming of Jesus Christ Can Be Judged

In order to prevent various arbitrary opinions harmful to the growth of spiritual life, our Saviour indicated some important signs through which we can sense the approach and beginning of the time for His second coming.

(1)   The first sign—an increase in catastrophes. Questioned by His disciples as to what kind of sign would precede His coming and the end of the world, He answered them with the following: "And you will hear of wars and rumors of wars. See that you are not troubled; for all these things must come to pass, but the end is not yet. For nation will rise against nation, and kingdom against kingdom. And there will be famines, pestilences, and earthquakes in various places. All these are the beginning of sorrows. Then they will deliver you up to tribulation and kill you, and you will be hated by all nations for My name's sake. And then many will be offended, will betray one another, and will hate one another. Then many false prophets will rise up and deceive many. . . . For then there will be great tribulation, such as has not been since the beginning of the world until this time, no,

nor ever shall be. And unless those days were shortened,
no flesh would be saved; but for the elect's sake those
days will be shortened" (Matt 24:6–11; 21–22).

(2)   The second sign—the preaching of the Gospel in all
the world. "And this gospel of the kingdom will be
preached in all the world as a witness to all the nations"
(Matt 24:14). The Antichrist shall come into the world
only when the preaching of the Gospel shall have been
spread over the whole universe, when all tribes and
peoples shall be enlightened with the light of Christian
teaching. St John of Damascus warns: "Jesus Christ will
come in order to accuse the anti-godly Hebrews [those
who did not receive Jesus as God but do receive the
imposter who calls himself God], after the Gospel has
been preached to all nations."[13]

(3)   The third sign—the lessening of faith and love among
people. "Because lawlessness will abound, the love of
many shall grow cold" (Matt 24:12). Then will follow
the "abomination of desolation," spoken of by Daniel
the prophet (Matt 24:15; see Daniel 9:27, 11:31). "Nevertheless, when the Son of Man comes, will He really find
faith on the earth?" (Luke 18:8). The primordial enemy,
Satan, sowing the weeds of falsehood and deceit before
the end of the world, shall direct all his means and powers in order to take by force and subjugate to his destructive rule all of those called to the kingdom of heaven.

(4)   The fourth sign—the conversion of Jews to Christ.
Thus in his Epistle to the Romans the Apostle Paul—
describing the special grace of God toward the pagans
who through faith were grafted from the wild to the

good olive tree, and inversely, the special severity of God's judgment toward the Jews in that they fell away from their native olive tree—pointed out that for Jews, in spite of this, it is by no means impossible or hopeless to again be grafted to their native olive tree (see Rom 11:22). Fixing his gaze into the distant future, Paul added these words: "For I do not desire, brethren, that you should be ignorant of this mystery, lest you should be wise in your own opinion, that blindness in part has happened to Israel until the fullness of the Gentiles has come in. And so all Israel will be saved, as it is written: 'The Deliverer will come out of Zion, And He will turn away ungodliness from Jacob'" (Rom 11:25–26).

(5) The fifth sign—the appearance of Antichrist. Finally, serving as the last and most precise sign of the approach of the second coming of Jesus Christ for judgment of the world, shall be the appearance of Antichrist. Under the special power of Satan, he will use all possible flattering and destructive means in order to shake or completely overthrow the kingdom of Christ, so unbearable to him since it is a kingdom of truth and good. In its stead, he will seek to erect and make firm his own murky, sinful kingdom, which will continue until it is destroyed by the coming of Christ.

CHAPTER TEN

The Coming of the Antichrist

Before the second coming of Christ, Christianity, spiritual knowledge, and morality will be in an impoverished state. "For false christs and false prophets will rise and show great signs and wonders to deceive, if possible, even the elect" (Matt 24:24). The Antichrist himself will produce numerous miracles, astonishing and satisfying the carnal wisdom and base desires of man. He will show them a sign from heaven for which they seek and crave. The holy Apostle Paul says that his coming will be accomplished through "the working of Satan, with all power, signs, and lying wonders, and with all unrighteous deception among those who perish, because they did not receive the love of the truth, that they might be saved" (2 Thess 2:9–10).

Seeing these miracles, mankind in its ignorance and carnal wisdom, will not stop to think; they will immediately accept these signs because of the kinship of their spirits, and in their blindness, will recognize and confess the actions of Satan as the greatest manifestation of the power of God. The Antichrist will be accepted very quickly and thoughtlessly. People will not realize that his miracles do not serve any good purpose, have no definite meaning, are alien to truth, and are simply a monstrous, malicious, senseless hoax. They are an intensive attempt to amaze, beguile, fool, perplex, obscure, and captivate through the fascination of elaborate, empty illusions.

It is not strange that the miracles of the Antichrist will be accepted rapturously and without question by apostates from Christianity, the enemies of truth and of God. They have prepared themselves for the open, active acceptance of the emissary and instrument of Satan, and his teachings and actions, by entering in advance into communion with Satan in spirit.

It is worthy of serious attention and sighing that the actions and miracles of the Antichrist will cause difficulties for the very elect of God. The reason for the strong influence of the Antichrist on mankind consists of his hellish cunning and hypocrisy, by which he will artfully conceal the most horrible evil—his unbridled and shameless audacity, the full cooperation of fallen spirits, and finally, the ability to work miracles, false miracles, but impressive.

Man's imagination is powerless to conceive of such a villain as the Antichrist will be. It is unnatural for the heart of man, even as depraved as it is, to believe the degree of evil which will be reached in the Antichrist. He will proclaim his worthiness just as his forerunners did, calling himself a preacher and restorer of the true knowledge of God. Those who do not understand Christianity will see in him a representative and champion of true religion, and will join him. He will boast that he is the promised Messiah. Having seen his glory, power, and gifted abilities, and the vast progress in worldly things, his supporters will praise him, serve him, and proclaim him as god. The Antichrist will appear meek, gracious, full of love and all virtues. He will be accepted as such and will be submitted to by those who accept as truth man's fallen truth, and have not renounced it for the truth of the Gospel.

The Antichrist will offer mankind the possibility of greater earthly well-being and prosperity, esteem, riches, splendor, bodily conveniences, and luxuries. Those who seek only the material will accept Antichrist and will proclaim him their master.

The Antichrist will present a disgraceful spectacle to mankind by a contrived theatrical display of astonishing miracles, unexplainable by present-day science; he will terrify all by the awesome wonders of his miracles, and will satisfy the vanity and pride of man through these miracles. All men guided by the light of their fallen nature, estranged from the guidance of the light of God, shall be captivated into obedience by the deceiver (see Rev 13:8).

The signs of the Antichrist will occur primarily in the skies for Satan is primarily in control of this realm. The signs will mainly influence the sense of sight, enchanting it and fooling it. St John the Theologian, contemplating the events in the world which are to precede its end, says that the Antichrist will perform great deeds, "so that he even makes fire come down from heaven on the earth in the sight of men" (Rev 13:13).

The Scriptures emphasize that this magnificent and fearful sight, occurring in the air, will be one of the more important signs of the Antichrist. These signs and spirits of the Antichrist will enhance his deceitful behavior and seduce most of mankind into following him.

The adversaries of the Antichrist will be regarded as troublemakers, enemies of social good and order, and will be subjected to hidden and open persecution, tortures, and execution. Evil spirits, sent over all the universe, will induce in men an exalted opinion of the Antichrist, and a general rapture and invincible attraction to him. The gravity of the last persecution against

Christians and the brutality of the persecutor are depicted in Holy Scripture. A definitive and decisive feature is the name given to this terrible man: he is called a *beast* (see Rev 13:1), just as the fallen angel was called *serpent* or a *dragon* (see Gen 3:1; Rev 12:3). All three names truly describe the character of both enemies of God. One acts more secretly, the other more openly; but to the *beast*, which has a similarity to all beasts, uniting in himself their diverse ferocity, the *dragon* gave "his power, his throne, and great authority" (Rev 13:2).

For the saints of God a horrible ordeal will begin. Craftiness, hypocrisy, and the miracles of the persecutor will intensify in order to seduce and deceive them; refined, fabricated, and fine-tuned by insidious inventiveness, the constraints, persecutions, and unlimited power of the torturer will place them in the most difficult situation. Their small numbers will seem insignificant before all mankind, and their opinion will be considered as nothing. General contempt, hatred, slander, oppression, and violent death will become their lot. The saints of God will be able to stand against the enemy of God and confess the Lord, Jesus Christ before him only with the special cooperation of God's grace and under its guidance.

St John the Theologian writes: "every spirit that does not confess that Jesus Christ has come in the flesh is not of God. And this is the spirit of the Antichrist, which you have heard was coming, and is now already in the world" (1 John 4:3).

Those who live with the spirit of the Antichrist cast off Christ, for they have accepted the Antichrist by their own spirit, entered into communion with him, subjugated themselves and bowed down to him in spirit, acknowledging him as their god. "For this reason God will send them strong delusion, that they should believe the lie, that they all may be condemned who did not believe the truth but had pleasure in unrighteousness" (2 Thess 2:11–12).

In His long-suffering, God is a just Judge. This patience shall be both a source of satisfaction (contentment) and an accusation and judgment of man's spirit. The Antichrist shall come in his own predetermined time. His coming shall be preceded by a general apostasy by the majority of Christians. By apostasy from Christ mankind shall be prepared for the acceptance of the Antichrist, and shall receive him in its spirit. Within the very tone of the spirit of mankind, there will arise a demand, an invitation to the Antichrist, sympathy for him, just as in the condition of a virulent malady, a thirst arises for a deadly drink to end the suffering.

The invitation is announced! The call echoes throughout mankind, expressing an insistent need for a genius who would raise material development and success to its highest degree and usher in well-being on earth, after which heaven becomes superfluous for man. The Antichrist will be the logical, just, natural result of the general moral and spiritual direction of mankind.[14]

CHAPTER ELEVEN

The Birth of Antichrist and His Acceptance by the Jews as the True Messiah

The Antichrist will be a real man, born of a supposed virgin, though in reality a fallen woman, as opposed to Jesus Christ, Who was born of the Most Pure Virgin Mary. Antichrist the man will be the son of evil, and as Hippolytus of Rome says, will be born of an unclean virgin, a Jewess, from the tribe of Dan. St John of Damascus says: "The devil himself shall not become a man, but a man will be born of fornication, and will adopt for himself all the activity of Satan; for God, foreseeing the future depravity of his will, shall permit Satan to enter into him. Born of a fornicator, he shall be raised secretly, shall be announced to all unexpectedly, and will ascend the throne."[15]

St Andrew of Caesarea writes, "The tribe of Dan is not listed with the others, for out of it will come the Antichrist; and instead of it the tribe of Levi is listed, which, as a priestly tribe is not entered in the list of tribes."[16]

After attaining a certain age, the Antichrist will appear in the world. As Jesus Christ appeared first of all to the Jews with His preaching, so the Antichrist, by descent an uncircumcised Jew, will come first to the Jews, and then will attract other peoples. Those Jews who do not believe in Christ will accept the Antichrist with great joy; they will believe him to be the Messiah, promised by the prophets. Concerning such a delusion of the unbelieving Jews the Lord said: "I have come in My Father's name, and you do not receive Me; if another comes in his own name, him you will receive" (John 5:43). The same thought is confirmed by St Paul: "because they did not receive the love of the truth, that they might be saved. And for this reason God will send them strong delusion, that they should believe the lie, that they all may be condemned who did not believe the truth but had pleasure in unrighteousness" (2 Thess 2:10–12). The holy Fathers, St John Chrysostom, St Cyril of Alexandria, and St John of Damascus, concur with these words of the Divine Scriptures. The last says: "The Jews did not receive our Lord Jesus Christ, the Son of God; but they will receive an impostor, who will call himself God." According to the teaching of the Word of God and the Fathers and Teachers of the Church, the Antichrist will be a man, who will appear in the world by the action of Satan and will act on earth under the direct influence of Satan.

In a sermon of Hippolytus of Rome, the Antichrist is represented as a visible, definite man. He will be "meek, quiet, courteous, impoverished; the people will see only his virtues and will select him as their king … saying within themselves, it is hardly possible to have found such a good and righteous man among our people. The Hebrews will think that he will want to reestablish their kingdom. After these things he will become proud in heart and will then be cruel, merciless, and barbarous."

CHAPTER TWELVE

The Antichrist Foretold

"Says the Lord Almighty. 'Behold, I will send you Elijah before the coming of the great and glorious day of the Lord'" (Mal 3:21–22 LXX). "'And I will give power to my two witnesses, and they will prophesy one thousand two hundred and sixty days, clothed in sackcloth.' These are the two olive trees and the two lampstands standing before the God of the earth" (Rev 11:3–4). "These have power to shut heaven, so that no rain falls in the days of their prophecy" (Rev 11:6). "And I will give power to my two witnesses, and they will prophesy" (Rev 11:3). "And if anyone wants to harm them, he must be killed ..." (Rev 11:5). "When they finish their testimony, the beast that ascends out of the bottomless pit will make war against them, overcome them, and kill them. And their dead bodies will lie in the street of the great city which spiritually is called Sodom and Egypt, where also our Lord was crucified. . . . those from the peoples ... will see their dead bodies three-and-a-half days, and not allow their dead bodies to be put into graves" (Rev 11:7–8). "Now after the three-and-a-half days the breath of life from God entered them, and they stood on their feet, and great fear fell on those who saw them" (Rev 11:11).

✿ Chapter Thirteen

The Actions and the Name of the Antichrist

Ten kings "shall arise, and after them another shall arise. He shall surpass all those before him in evils, and he shall humble three kings. He will speak extremely arrogant words and wear down the saints of the Most High" (Dan 7:24–25); "who opposes and exalts himself above all that is called God or that is worshipped, so that he sits as God in the temple of God, showing himself that he is God" (2 Thess 2:4). "The coming of the lawless one is according to the working of Satan, with all power, signs, and lying wonders, and with all unrighteous deception among those who perish" (2 Thess 2:9–10).

The luminaries of the Church, the holy Fathers, unanimously confirm that nobody can know the name of the Antichrist, for the ways of the Lord are past finding out, and His judgments are unsearchable. It is known from Revelation, that the Antichrist will give an inscription of his name to all his followers.

"He causes all, both small and great, rich and poor, free and slave, to receive a mark on their right hand or on their foreheads, that no one may buy or sell except one who has the mark or the name of the beast, or the number of his name. Here is wisdom. Let him who has understanding calculate the number of the beast, for it is the number of a man: His number is 666." (Rev 13:16–18).

St Hippolytus of Rome says, "The Antichrist shall become a king, and will demand worship from all, and those who submit will be sealed with his sign, and those not wanting to obey him he will debilitate with suffering and countless severe tortures and executions, and will put Elijah and Enoch to death."

The Antichrist will continue to rule a year and another two years and yet a half year. "He shall be given authority for a time, times, and half a time" (Dan 7:25).

"But the woman was given two wings of a great eagle, that she might fly into the wilderness to her place, where she is nourished for a time and times and half a time, from the presence of the serpent" (Rev 12:14). "Then the woman fled into the wilderness, where she has a place prepared by God, that they should feed her there one thousand two hundred and sixty days" (Rev 12:6), "and they will tread the holy city underfoot for forty-two months" (Rev 11:2).

"And then the lawless one will be revealed, whom the Lord will consume with the breath of His mouth and destroy with the brightness of His coming" (2 Thess 2:8).

"Then the king shall do according to his will. He will be exalted himself and magnified above every god, and speak arrogant words. He shall prosper till the wrath has been accomplished, for it is to be ended. He shall not regard any gods of his fathers, nor the desire of women, nor shall he regard any god; for he shall exalt himself above them all" (Dan 11:36–37). "Let no one deceive you by any means; for that Day will not come unless the falling away comes first, and the man of sin is revealed, the son of perdition, who opposes and exalts himself above all that is called God or that is worshiped, so that he sits as God in the temple of God, showing himself that he is God" (2 Thess 2:3–4).

"He performs great signs, so that he even makes fire come down from heaven on the earth in the sight of men. And he deceives those who dwell on the earth by those signs which he was granted to do in the sight of the beast, telling those who dwell on the earth to make an image to the beast who was wounded by the sword and lived" (Rev 13:13–14).

The persecution of the saints [all true believers]: "So I kept looking, and that horn made war with the saints and prevailed against them" (Dan 7:21). "It was granted to him to make war with the saints and to overcome them. And authority was given him over every tribe, tongue, and nation" (Rev 13:7).

CHAPTER FOURTEEN

The Seal of Antichrist

The Antichrist shall stamp with his own seal all those who shall have made their obeisance to him. There is very little said concerning the seal of the Antichrist in the Holy Scriptures or in the Fathers of the Church. St John the Theologian writes in Revelation: The Antichrist "causes all, both small and great, rich and poor, free and slave, to receive a mark on their right hand or on their foreheads, and that no one may buy or sell except one who has the mark or the name of the beast, or the number of his name" (Rev 13:16–17).

These words clearly show that the seal of Antichrist will be a special imprint, or a sign on the right hand, and that this seal will have a threefold appearance: a plain imprint or seal, the imprint of the name of Antichrist, and finally, the number of the name on the right hand or forehead. St Andrew of Caesarea and St Hippolytus indicate the signs of the seal of the Antichrist. St Andrew first explains the seal of the Antichrist in an allegorical manner, saying that the seal on the right hand is the denial of good, and the one on the forehead is a denial of truth and a service of flattery.[17] Secondly, the seal of the Antichrist will also have an outer sign—it will contain the number of the name of Antichrist, 666, but the grace of God has not given us to know this name. The same clue is given by St Hippolytus. Therefore, the seal of the Antichrist is a special mark on the forehead and/or on the right hand. It is also such a mark that it could be placed on every other part of the body, but as St Ephraim the Syrian explains, it will be on the right hand in order to hinder the followers of the Antichrist from using their right hands to make the sign of the cross of the Lord, which is especially fearful for the Antichrist.

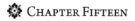
The Miracles of the Antichrist

There is clear evidence of the miracles of the Antichrist in Scripture, the works of the holy Fathers, and early catechetical books. The Lord Jesus Christ Himself says that the servants of the Antichrist shall show great signs and wonders; inasmuch that, if it were possible they shall deceive the very elect (see Matt 24:24). St John the Theologian says that one of these servants of the Antichrist, his forerunner, shall do especially great wonders (see Rev 13:13–15). And the Apostle Paul says that the coming of the Antichrist shall be with all power and signs and lying wonders (see 2 Thess 2:9).

According to the testimony of the Fathers of the Church, the Antichrist will actually perform miracles. We read in the *Great Catechism* that the Antichrist shall come and shall perform miracles by illusions, falsehoods, and sorcery. St Cyril of Jerusalem warns: "The Antichrist shall seduce by means of many false signs and miracles."

The miracles performed by the Antichrist will be innumerable and diverse as St Paul the apostle describes them, full of all power and signs and lying wonders. The Fathers foresee that people will think that even Christ could not have been able to create as many miracles as will be performed by His adversary, and they depict the miraculous actions of the Antichrist in the most clear and detailed terms. St Hippolytus teaches that the Antichrist will cleanse lepers, drive out devils, raise the enfeebled, will communicate with those far away as well as those close by, raise the dead, produce mountains before the eyes of beholders, will walk on the sea with feet unwet, bring down fire from heaven, will make day dark, and night day, transfigure the sun as he desires, as well as the moon, and will show that all the elements, the earth and the seas, will seem to all those watching to be obedient to him through the power of his illusions.[18]

In order to understand these unusual powers of the Antichrist, it is necessary to remember that his coming will be the doing of Satan (see 2 Thess 2:9), who at that time will be permitted by God to act with the greatest freedom, for Satan shall be let loose near the end of the world, even though for only a short time (see Rev 20:3). Blessed Augustine says that the loosed Satan, who is to act through the Antichrist, shall assume such power, which he never had before.[19] We do know from Scripture that Satan, when permitted by God, was able not only to smite Job with pus "from head to foot," but he also brought down fire "from heaven and burned up the sheep, and likewise consumed the shepherds," and sent "a great wind from the desert" which destroyed the whole house, in which were the children of Job (see Job 2:7; 1:16–19).

Therefore it is not surprising that near the end of the world the enemy of the race of man will produce through the Antichrist even greater deeds, in order to captivate people into worshiping him; for the honor which people will lavish on the Antichrist, will really belong to him whom the Antichrist shall bear within him. The coming of the Antichrist shall occur with all power and signs and false miracles.

According to commentaries of the holy Fathers, the Antichrist will be a great magician and sorcerer. Satan, who will reside in him from birth, will, through him, arrange false miracles; some imaginary, others naturally, as the Egyptian sages did at one time. St Andrew of Caesarea says: "It is written that demons often spoke by means of statues and pictures, waters and trees, through the statue of Apollo, and others. Also, by means of dead bodies, as, for instance, Simon the Magician, in the Apostle Peter's presence, showed to the Romans a dead body which moved. The Apostle exposed him, showing how the dead arise whom he himself resurrected"[20] (13th word on Rev). The Antichrist shall also pretend to die, and will then arise—by such indicated miracles he will astonish the whole world!

CHAPTER SIXTEEN

The Disparagement of Divine Law by the Antichrist; The Persecutions and Tortures of Those Confessing Christ

The Antichrist will be an obstinate enemy of Christ. He will disparage all of Christ's actions and teachings, and will criticize miracles, and will attempt to ruin God's Law; he will renounce anointing with holy oil, baptism, Communion, and the remaining sacraments. The holy martyr Hippolytus in his discourse about the end of the world says: "During the time of the Antichrist the offering of the bloodless sacrifice to God shall be halted; God's churches will be demolished, they shall be turned into dens for robbers and indecent stables; psalm chanting shall not be heard, for every rank and all church splendor shall become extinct." St John Chrysostom says: "When he appears, he will order nothing that is right, only everything that is criminal and illegal."[21]

The Antichrist will command all to be circumcised and to worship on Saturdays. Being accepted by Jewish people as the Messiah, he himself will accept everything that is Jewish; they will not believe in Jesus Christ as the Son of God, so their messiah, the Antichrist, shall disparage and hate Him. "Who is a liar," exclaims St John the Theologian, "but he who denies that Jesus is the Christ? He is the antichrist who denies the Father and the

64

Son. Whosoever denies the Son does not have the Father either" (1 John 2:22–23).

Having called himself God, the Antichrist will have over himself a kind of strong god, that is the devil. The holy Prophet Daniel witnesses: "he shall honor a god of fortresses, and a god his fathers did not know he shall honor with gold and silver, and with precious stones and desirable things" (Dan 11:38).

CHAPTER SEVENTEEN

The Construction by the Antichrist of His Altar in the Temple at Jerusalem

E noch and the Prophet Elijah shall fight against the Antichrist in Jerusalem; there "the beast that ascends out of the bottomless pit will make war against them, overcome them, and kill them. And their dead bodies will lie in the street of the great city which spiritually is called Sodom and Egypt, where also our Lord was crucified" (Rev 11:7, 8). These words tell us that the Antichrist, having been received by the Jews as the Messiah, an earthly king, will establish his throne in spiritual Sodom, that will be in Jerusalem, on the throne of David. According to the testimony of the Apostle, he will restore the Jerusalem Temple and will sit in it as God.[22]

The holy Fathers Cyril of Jerusalem, Gregory, Hippolytus, and John Chrysostom designate the church of God and the holy place as the temple of Solomon. St John of Damascus notes, "Antichrist shall erect his throne not in our temple, but in the Jewish one, for he came not to us, but to the Jews, and not for Christ, but against Him."

St Andrew says, "He will found his kingdom in Jerusalem, according to the example of David, whose son, in flesh, was Jesus, our true God; and he will do this in order to assure all that he is Christ, fulfilling prophetical words: 'I shall raise up the fallen tabernacle of David, and I shall rebuild its ruins and repair its damages'" (Amos 9:11).[23]

The Lord, too, spoke of the throne of the Antichrist: you will "see the 'abomination of desolation,' spoken of by Daniel the prophet, standing in the holy place" (Matt 24:15; see Dan 9:27).

CHAPTER EIGHTEEN

The Terrible State of the World and All Mankind during the Reign of the Antichrist

As the Word of God teaches, so also the holy Fathers and teachers of the Church clearly and definitely say that before the Antichrist the state of mankind will be extremely fallen, that at that time there will be great affliction, such as has not been seen from the beginning of the world till now, and that finally, unless those days should be shortened, then should no flesh be saved. Not only will people in those days suffer "great persecution and cruel torture," but even animals equally with people, and maybe because of people, will be subjected to innumerable sufferings. Finally, even visible nature will suffer various unnatural changes and upheaval and will suffer, not willingly, but because it was made subject to the vanity of man, its ruler and king.

Calamities will overtake the earth in the latter days. Some will be the work of the Antichrist, while others will be punishment by the Almighty right hand of God for man's impiety and apostasy. Especially difficult and distressful will be the state of the elect of God, who will not submit to the Antichrist. All the ferocities of the man of evil will be turned chiefly on them. Then there will be great persecution and fierce torture for all Orthodox Christians living in the faith, who do not obey the Antichrist's will and accept the mark on their forehead and right hand. They will hide from the Antichrist in secret and remote places, in the hills and deserts, but the servants of the Antichrist will search them out even there and will return them to worship the enemy of Christ, and he will coerce them to deny Christ.

A special affliction of people during the reign of the Antichrist will be hunger. At first, this will be visited on those who will not worship the Antichrist and will not accept his seal. St John the Theologian says that no one will be able to buy or to sell, save he that has the mark, or the name of the beast, or the number of his name (see Rev 13:17), for the Antichrist will place merciless inspectors everywhere, and only he who has the mark of the torturer on his forehead and right hand will be able to buy a little food from the spare quantities that will be available. This circumstance shall cause many to accept the rule of the servants of the Antichrist: "Come all and see his strength and power. He will grant you life and make gifts of wine, priceless riches, great honors, and because of the scarcity in food supplies, all will come to him and worship him, and will accept his seal, and the flatterer will give them a little food for the sake of the foul seal."

The visible advantages of those who had worshiped the Antichrist, over those who had not, will not last long. Soon, by God's command, seven angels shall pour out seven vials upon the earth, sea, rivers, fountains of water, the sun, the throne of the beast, the great river Euphrates, and finally into the air (see Rev 16), defeating the rule of the Antichrist and those who abandoned themselves to him. By the will of the Lord all of nature will be armed against the Antichrist and his worshipers. When the believers in the Antichrist become exposed to the varied calamities from the punishing right arm of the Most High—especially when they begin to feel hunger and thirst—then they shall come to the Antichrist crying out with sickly voices: "Give us food and drink for we fade away from hunger and illness; command the sky to give us rain, and drive away from us the man-eating beasts." Then the adversary will answer, reproaching them in great perplexity, saying: "Where shall I get the food and drink for you? The sky does not give its rain, the earth does not want to give its grain, where shall I get the foods to give you?" Then, hearing the words of this flatterer, the wretched ones will discover that he is the evil adversary, and will begin to painfully cry and sob, hit themselves in the face, tear their hair, and scratch their faces with their nails. They will cry out: "O the plight, O the betrayal of the flatterer, O the fateful investments, O the fall of the great one, how were we seduced, how were we led to the flatterer, how were we caught alive by his nets! Why did we revile the preachers when we heard them? How did we hear the Holy Scriptures and not understand them?"[24] The recognition of guilt, however, will not ease the condition of the distressed, for, though greatly desiring to hide, "they will not be able to run from the path of the adversary, but carrying around his mark, they will be better known and recognizable to him." Enduring the just anger of God, they will suffer even more from the thought that this mark will remain their eternal inheritance, in witness of their apostasy from God, from Christ the Saviour, and therefore, after their sufferings on earth, they can still expect eternal tortures in hell. According to the teaching of the holy Fathers which is in keeping with the Word of God, for those who have fallen away from Christ and accepted the mark of the Antichrist, there is no salvation. "These will find themselves no mercy in the day of judgment, having worshipped the Antichrist as the Holy God, they shall have no part in Christ's coming, but will be put into Gehenna together with the serpent."[25]

After this it will not be surprising that "there will be darkness over mankind, tears on tears, and sorrow on sorrow"; from such sufferings "pleasant faces and appearances shall wither away, they will look like the dead, and the graces of women will fade away; and gold and silver will be discarded everywhere, and nobody will take it or gather it, but all will become an abomination."[26]

The beast "shall devour all the earth, and trample and break it in pieces." "He shall stretch out his hand upon the land, and the land of Egypt will not escape. He shall gain control over the hidden stores of gold and silver, and over all the precious things of Egypt, and of the Libyans and Ethiopians in their strongholds" (Dan 7:23; 11:42–43).

"The ten horns which you saw are ten kings who have received no kingdom as yet, but they receive authority for one hour as kings with the beast. These are of one mind, and they will give their power and authority to the beast. These will make war with the Lamb, and the Lamb will overcome them" (Rev 17:12–14).

"Now when the thousand years have expired, Satan will be released from his prison and will go out to deceive the nations which are in the four corners of the earth, Gog and Magog, to gather them together to battle, whose number is as the sand of the sea. They went up on the breadth of the earth and surrounded the camp of the saints and the beloved city. And fire came down from God out of heaven and devoured them. The devil, who deceived them, was cast into the lake of fire and brimstone where the beast and the false prophet are. And they will be tormented day and night forever and ever" (Rev 20:7–10).

Chapter Nineteen

Posthumous Prophecies of Our Holy Father Nilus the Myrrh-streamer of Mount Athos

Foreword

The *Posthumous Prophecies of St Nilus the Myrrh-streamer* describes the miraculous events which occurred on the Holy Mountain between the years 1813 and 1819 when the Athonite hermit St Nilus the Myrrhstreamer (+ 1651) made a number of posthumous revelations to a monk of Mount Athos concerning the Antichrist, the decline of monastic life, and gave an understanding of the true path of salvation. The saint communicated through Theophan that he was being sent by God, like Noah to the pre-flood people, and Jonah to Nineveh, to proclaim that God is ready to accept the repentance of even the most grievous sinners, just as while suspended on the Cross, He was ready to accept the repentance of Judas whose conversion He awaited, and whose destruction He mourned.

Since grievous times are foreseen, of which the Lord says: "when the Son of Man comes, will He really find faith on the earth?" (Luke 18:8), the saint made known to those searching for salvation that they need not be troubled and fearful, but need to try to guard their faith in God inviolate and pure. The saint also foretold of the mark of the Antichrist; the worldwide anarchy, which should precede the coming of the Antichrist; the coercion of poor farmers; the degree of depravity of the later generations; the preaching of Enoch and Elijah against the seal of the Antichrist, and their call to people to sign themselves with the sign of the cross, and much more in a similar vein. These "posthumous revelations" unceasingly tell us of the struggle against Satan.

Fearful are the signs of God's anger, but alas, our insensibility abandons everything to forgetfulness! We firmly confess and deeply believe in the truth of the heavenly appearances of St Nilus and the godliness of his sayings, in spite of the fact that the form in which Theophan transmitted the content of his conversations with the saint is quite incomplete. Some parts are difficult to understand, there is much repetition, there are omissions; but with an attentive examination and with the help of God, we can discern the grace-filled thoughts which were uttered by the mouth of Theophan. For the humble, wise searcher of truth these revelations will serve as unquestionable proof of the godliness of their origin, and the humble-minded will not be led astray by the simple style used by Theophan in setting down what he was told by St Nilus, for he will remember that the Apostles too were fishermen and by their simple teaching the Gentiles were converted.

God Sent Me to You, As the Tablets to Moses

> "Do not reprove evil men, so they may not hate you; Reprove a wise man, and he will love you. Give the opportunity to a wise man, and he will be wiser; Instruct a righteous man, and he shall continue to receive it" (Prov 9:8–9).

Now I have presented your life before you, but have you been receptive to all of this? Or will my words vanish as nothing? But, since these words are not my own but those of Him Who sent me, is it possible that they will be in vain? If you will not have the judgment to think of yourself, my words to you will be wasted, and later you will have no answer. If you will not have the judgment to appraise my words, they will be wasted on you, and you will be without defense.

God, knowing the sinfulness of man and the inclination of people to evil, sent Moses to them with the tablets containing the ten commandments; since Moses was slow of speech, his brother Aaron recited to the people the commandments written on the tablets, conveying them through speech for man's understanding. In the same manner I have been sent to you by God, as a tablet (to the monk Theophan), tongue-tied as to grammatical speech, that you might transmit this to your advisor, Father Gerasim, as did Moses to Aaron, and that your advisor might set it down in writing for the understanding of the listeners as did Aaron.

Yes, let Father Gerasim transmit this, but concisely and attentively, for much wordiness causes contradictions and this causes great confusion among people.

Amen, amen, I say to you, contradictions cause harm, not benefits. After he has transmitted my words to people clearly, let him go where he pleases, for they will try to obliterate you from the face of the earth, to kill both of you, and will try to prove that my words are a diabolic prattle.

Moses, having accepted the tablets, related them to Aaron, and Aaron retold them to the people; but they heard only with their ears, and then placed the tablets in the dust under their feet regarding them as nothing. So they will consider my words, which I have told you.

Prophetic Characteristics of People before the End of the World

For these reasons I tell you ... When the seventh number of years shall pass, and five more rising halfway toward the eighth, there, halfway to the fifth number, what confusion there will be from the fourth to the fifth (after the passing of 7,400 years from the creation of the world, then between the fourth and fifth centuries, or, during the course of the present twentieth century [The first printing of Archimandrite Panteleimon's book *Ray of Light* was in 1946.]). What plundering there will then be! What sensualism, adultery, incest, and debauchery will then take place!

To what decadence will people then descend, to what corruption through fornication? Then will there be confusion and a great struggle for power (the whole world will encounter revolutions and the struggle of parties); there will be interminable wrangling with no beginning and no end.

Later an eighth (ecumenical) council shall meet, in order to appraise the disorder and to impart well-being to the good, evil to the wicked ... The farmer separates wheat from chaff. The wheat is for man, and the chaff for animals. We maintain that the good will be separated from the evil doers—the right-believing from the heretics, and for a short time people will see peace restored (This is also spoken of in Byzantine prophecies).

Later they will again change their good outlook, will turn to evil with the same evil as those who are perishing. The father and mother, and mother and son, shall not recognize even the crown of marriage. They will have the same fate, one general fall into perdition, just like Sodom and Gomorrah (there will not be found even five righteous people). Then brother will take his sister as wife, a mother will take a son as a husband, sons will murder fathers to commit adultery with mothers; and a whole host of evils will become the custom. To the extent that people become engrossed in evil, so too will grief come upon them.

The more calamities afflict them, the more evil will they become; instead of repenting, they will be angered at God. The evil deeds of people will surpass those of people at the time of the flood. All will speak only of evil, plan only evil, consent to evil, meet others only for evil; every person's works will be only evil ones, with general plundering and oppression, aloofness, and disunion. At the same time, they will think that the doer of evil is being saved. Then they will become greedy (i.e., they will have financial resources, but will complain of the lack of them). They will lend money out at interest, and will receive interest on interest. They will beg in order to feed themselves, and will cry that they have no food. Their main aim will be the gathering of capital in order to have more possessions; as much as their greed will increase, so too will calamities mount in the world.

That is why I say to you: when four quarter centuries will pass, what will be the state of monastic life then? If three more quarter centuries will pass: meaning seven, and five rising halfway to eight, there in the center of the five, what confusion will occur from the fourth to the fifth?

Commentary

The saint said this to Theophan in the year 1817 from the birth of Christ; 7,325 years from the creation of the world according to Orthodox teaching. Therefore, the saint says: when four quarters of a century will pass, (100 years), and the year 7,425 will arrive, what will become of monastic life? (Everybody is familiar with what happened to Russian monasteries in 1917. Before the communist revolution there were in Russia: 529 men's monasteries and 456 convents with 10,998 monks, 15,000 nuns, 10,203 male novices, and 55,450 female novices. There were 53,546 Orthodox churches, 22,850 Orthodox chapels, 37,641 parish schools, 28 teachers' schools, 4 religious academies, 57 seminaries, and 266 church schools. Before the revolution there were 130 million faithful Russian Orthodox people, and today what of all of this has survived and escaped unscathed?) Now, if three more quarter centuries pass, (75 years), and we come to the 7,500th year of creation: "the number 7 of years added to 5" (or seven thousand years and 500 years), "rising halfway to the eighth" (when we reach the middle of the eighth age), then here, "in the middle of the fifth" (1942) "what confusion there will be" (from the 4th [1892] to the 5th [1992]!).

We understand St Nilus to mean that from the 4th to the 5th means from the years 7,400 to 7,500 AD from creation. St Nilus said the above to monk Theophan in 1817/7,325. State of monastic life 100 years later 1917/7,425. The middle of the eighth age 1942/7,450. What confusion there will be from the 4th to the 5th century (from 1892 to 1992)1992/7,500.

The Prophecy on the Increase of Poverty; Persecution of Poor Peasants, Their Resettlements; The Grain Monopoly Preceding the Birth of the Antichrist

The poverty-ridden will be persecuted by reason of provincial expenses. (Evidently here we may understand the communist tendency to form collective farms, in order to expropriate private property from all, even the poor. The calamities described are fulfilled exactly by the godless communists.) The poor, however, not being able to pay their share of the demanded provincial expenses shall be forced to leave their places and to try to find others, in order to find rest and peace there, but again they will find the same troubles, only worse. Finally, not having enough strength to move to another region, they will go to the cemeteries and say: "Take us too; you have rested long enough, let us rest a short while, until the last judgment awakens us." They will say much more to the cemeteries, and the groans of the poor will rise like incense before God. Seeing such sufferings, God will provide (a harvest) for the whole world, and the poor, seeing such good, will happily praise God for the harvest; and when the fruits will be gathered into the barns, the covetous one will come there and carry off all the grain into his (collective) grain bins, and will issue an order, that he who demands grain would come to him, and receive as much as he wants. Then the beggars will begin to go to the greedy one for grain (i.e., the peasants will buy their own grain from the monopoly).

The greedy one will then receive double the price for the grain than it cost a year earlier; the poor, seeing that the covetous one has turned even God's blessing into an expensive item, shall grumble at God; all, small and great, poor and rich, will grumble, and the latter more than the poor, for the poor are alien to greed. If they have two of some item, they keep one and give the other away out of a sense of duty; and if they have but one, even that is given away of necessity; and if they have none, even then they praise God. The covetous will imagine that the poor one has possessions and will begin to oppress the poor, in order to take the very last item from him. He will search for the slightest reason to oppress him. Yes, he will oppress him, but how?—he will take everything the poor man has by taking him to court; and if he has nothing, he will oppress him through jail, where he will weary him for not having anything to pay for his freedom. The usurer will visit the prison and torment the poor one in order to receive payments on the pretext that they are necessary for local expenses; his aim, however, is to receive his interest on the gold, which he has loaned at a percentage for local expenses; and this is why he tries to get more than necessary for his interest. (Under "usurers" one should understand bankers, who with their financial nets have enmeshed almost all of Europe and the world.)

Where shall the usurer get his bounty? The usurer wants to increase his income from the poor, but the poor do not even have enough to eat, and he, though rich, tries to confiscate something ... The beggar is at a loss to find anything that he might give to the usurer, and the latter does not know what he can take from the beggar. If things remain so, he will suffer a loss (i.e., the gold given out at interest, will not grow), for the poor have nothing that might be taken.

The usurer notices the rich man who walks around in torn clothing (i.e., the one who has loaned out his capital at interest for local expenses, and through the poverty of the peasants did not receive his profit), and he also sees the beggar (i.e., the peasant), walking around in clean clothing; and the usurer shall pity the rich man, not the poor one, since he wears clean clothing. The usurer does not understand that the clean clothing of the beggar symbolizes his pure heart, for in it he has not the cunningness by which to pretend that he has nothing to wear.

The rich man has what he needs ... and has become evil, keeping his heart in rags, just like his clothing. Such has been and will be the rich man's heart; but the heart of the poor shines. Which poor man's heart will shine?—only his who is forbearing and will endure the usurer (not become angry at his unjust persecution).

Blessed is he who will endure everything the usurer does to him, for at the time of the Judgment before the fearful tribunal he will be acknowledged "as a brother of the Fearful Judge." He will say: "inasmuch as you did it to one of the least of these My brethren, you did it to Me" (Matt 25:40). Do you see, do you hear? How does He regard the poor at the Last Judgment? He says: "the least of these My brethren."

O usurer! Piratical is your soul! How long will you torture the poor? At some time in the future you will hear the terrible pronouncement, spoken to you: "Depart from Me, you cursed, into the everlasting fire" (Matt 25:41). You are preparing it for yourself; but, tell me, if you know the means by which you are preparing it. You do not know, therefore listen and examine the deeds by which you prepare it.

The preparation (of everlasting fire for yourself) is care, worry, and the gathering of riches. (Understood here are the cares which stifle the growth of spiritual strivings.) You prepare (the fire) for yourself by worrying only about worldly material things. You prepare it by having your whole attention on gathering the treasures of the world into your treasure house; and what are the treasures you discover you have been piling up?—envy, evil design, resentment, and enmity.

Yes, you have grasped for riches, and ended with what? Avarice, usury, and extortion from the poor. Yes, you have acquired treasure, and ended with what? Fornication, adultery, sodomy, a dissipating gluttony, insatiable plundering, and dissolute drunkenness. Yes, you have attracted conceited pride by your arrogant self-esteem and haughtiness. Yes, you have acquired negligent sloth by your carelessness with the distracted despair of cowardice and ungodly forgetfulness. Yes, you have gathered cruelty, cowardice, censure, and anger against the poor. Yes, you have accumulated wordiness, evil gossip, blame, by which you judge that one is harmful, another is despicable, and you pretend to seem better than all.

So it is, that then (during the time before the Antichrist), all will think much about themselves, and aside from that will censure one another. The extortioner will blame the poor and say, "the poor have money"; and because the latter will not pay his annual payment, the usurer will begin to jail the poor and torment him, and strip him, taking all of his silver and gold, in order to gather interest for his money.

However, the poor, seeing that the extortioner tortures them, will also begin to save and accumulate silver and gold as a reserve for the extortioner. The poor will gather money for the extortioner, but in so doing he himself will be seduced (by greed), and will begin to accumulate for himself; having gathered a surplus, he will desire to double his surplus, and when he succeeds, will want to quadruple it. Suddenly, he dies, departs this life, and finds himself in hell, while his body is buried according to the custom of the land.

Little by little the poor forget Christ in their greed for gold. It is because of you, the usurer, that the beggar overemphasized gold in order not to be jailed, and while gathering it, dies, opening his eyes in hell; and you, seeing that the beggar did leave some savings, censure him and all the poor, that they have savings. Because you humiliate the poor before others though you are the cause of his censure, you too shall be humiliated by the Just Judge at His judgment, and He will say to you: "Inasmuch as you did it to one of the least of these My brethren, you did it to Me" (Matt 25:40).

You, poor, why are you on a course of soul-destruction (i.e., the avaricious grubbing for money)? You have passed your whole life without avariciousness and God did not allow your destruction; and, today, at the sight of coercion by the usurer, and fascinated by the greed of gain, you became one with the usurer, and have made your soul leprous as did Geza. All of your life you enlightened your soul without greed, and, now when the usurer attacked, you became frightened of his coercion and began to practice usury together with him. For this reason you became equal to him.

Greed is the path to destruction; lack of greed is the path to salvation. You become avaricious and salvation is lost. Due to avarice, the salvation of mankind is imperiled by dangerous destruction. This, cursed avarice, will finally bring misfortune into the world, and will destroy the world's well-being. We repeat: the world will forget what well-being is, and misfortune will reign everywhere. This cursed greed of gain has and will establish discord in the world. But avarice will especially be a menace to monastic life, where this curse has begun to flourish to such an extent, along with the dissension that it causes, that it threatens to ruin monastic life itself. For blissful monasticism is now almost destroyed! Not only is monastic life disorganized, but the whole world is in confusion from the curse of avarice.

The Root of Evil Is Avarice, or Love of Money

Avarice is the forerunner of the Antichrist. The Holy Spirit, through the prophets, prophesied the economy of the incarnation of Christ; they announced the Truth to the world. On the other hand avarice brought falsehood into the world. Untruth will lead to the incarnation of destruction, when great calamity will come upon the world. As the word of the prophets foretold the economy of the incarnation of salvation, so, too, the increase in cares involving the acquisition of property and income is a portent of the nearness of the incarnation of the kingdom of destruction in the world, of the birth of the Antichrist, who will be a completely diabolic vessel, and be destruction incarnate.

Just as the Forerunner preached baptism by the Truth, and by this converted people to the way of salvation, so conversely, man's many preoccupations shall darken his feelings and make him insensible to salvation. Because of a preoccupation with bodily cares people will not be concerned for their salvation; they will feel neither the desire for the future eternal life, nor the fear of eternal judgment.

In this manner people will lose feeling (the feeling of internal, spiritual sight, the method by which we achieve higher knowledge), and will not be able to perceive God. They will enter into drinking and eating of fine foods and surrounding themselves with the most beautiful buildings. In these pleasures they will abandon themselves to their bodily senses, to pleasing only the flesh, as if building it up for an eternal festive celebration. Since they will entertain only their carnal senses, it is only good food that they will perceive, and for such things will they strive. Through such proclivity toward carnal uncleanliness, people will become abominable to God. Yes, God will abhor them, as He abhorred the antediluvian people, but at least He showed mercy to them, through the ark of repentance. God desired that the people of old, observing the building of the ark, would repent; but they directed their feelings toward the carnal, became unfeeling toward God and the ark, and could not sense the meaning of the ark. This insensitivity led them into the depths of the waters.

Antichrist Will Be Born When the World Will Become Spiritually Impoverished and When Worldwide Anarchy Begins

The Universal Reign of Antichrist

The Antichrist will be born of an unclean, wanton maid. All debaucheries will be united within this maid, and she will be a treasure house of fornication. Every evil of the world, every uncleanness, every sin will be embodied in her. Through her conceiving from secret wantonness, all sins will be combined in a womb of uncleanness and will be brought to life together with the spiritual impoverishment of the world. When the world will be deprived of the grace of the Most Holy Spirit, then the Antichrist will come to life in the womb of the unclean, from the most filthy and impure woman to have lived, though she will appear as a virgin. Conceived from such secret and unnatural wantonness, the offspring will be the container of every evil, as opposed to the way in which Christ was the ideal of every good quality, and His most pure Mother was the ideal of womanhood.

This offspring will be born when the world becomes destitute of virtues. What kind of poverty will overtake the world? There are many forms of poverty which will surround and gradually encompass the world. Firstly, love, harmony, and chastity will diminish in the world. Secondly, every settlement and city will be deprived of its leadership. Authorities will leave the cities, villages, and districts, so that not one leader will be found in a city, village, or district. So, too, the Church will lack spiritual leadership. After this impoverishment "the love of many will grow cold" (Matt 24:12). "He who now restrains will do so until he is taken out of the way" (2 Thess 2:7), and the unclean will be born from the womb of impurity. Later, this unclean birth will produce signs and wonders through demonic illusions.

The world will imagine that this antichrist is meek and humble at heart, but in reality he will be a fox at heart, and a wolf in soul; the confusion of people will be his food. When people become converted (that is perish), then the Antichrist will be satisfied.

The confusion of people will lead to censure, envy, rancor, hate, hostility, greed, sodomy, forgetfulness of faith, adultery, and praise of fornication. These evils will be food for the Antichrist. As bread for Christ was the fulfillment of the will of His heavenly Father, so food for the Antichrist shall be the fulfillment of the will of his father, Satan.

The Antichrist will be made the head of cities, villages, and districts when there are no longer any leaders for these places. Then he will seize authority over the world, will become the director of the world, and will also begin to rule over man's senses. People will believe everything he says, since he will act as a lone ruler and autocrat for the elimination of salvation. People, having become vessels of the devil, will develop the utmost trust toward the Antichrist and will make him a universal monarch and autocrat. He will be the instrument of the devil in his last attempt to annihilate Christianity from the face of the earth. Spiritually doomed, people will think that he is Christ the Saviour and that he will arrange their salvation. Then the Gospel of the Church be held in disdain.

After this, when evil brings great calamity to the world, fearful signs will occur. Terrible hunger will come and the world will experience a great insatiability for food. In comparison to the amount of food a person eats today, he will then eat seven times more and not be satisfied. (Evidently, the perversion of spiritual capabilities will cause man's material needs to be perverted and induce an abnormal appetite for food.)

Then a great disaster will occur worldwide. Then the greedy will open their greedy storehouses, i.e., capitalism will be abolished, property will be made equal, on the principle of socialism. Then gold will be worthless, like manure along the road.

The Spirit of Christ and the Spirit of Antichrist

Then the evil of the world will be born in the impure womb of the virgin of evil, who will give birth to the Antichrist. As a result of the iniquitous deeds of the world, the grace of the Holy Spirit, which had been maintaining the world, will depart from it, according to the words and "I will have not doings with their elect" (Ps 140:4 LXX).[27] Then the spirit of the Antichrist will become incarnate. That spirit which already moves in the world will become a person who will be the most defiled of all men and the perfect vessel of the devil even from his mother's womb, that is he will be born of an evil whore although externally she will appear like a virgin (morally).

Yes, evil will be incarnate (the Antichrist will be born) without any masculine seed. Yes, he will be born of seed, but without man's sowing, but will be born through artificial insemination. (Artificial insemination is already practiced with horses and cattle.)[28] What then is immaterial seed? The immaterial seed (of the Antichrist) is anger, care, worry, and greed. However, there are various kinds of cares; not every care is destructive and not all lack of care is good. It is most important for man is the care for his own salvation.

The salvation of man is found in love, meekness, chastity, absence of greed, virginal purity, righteousness, and merciful kindness—the "oil" of man's salvation (as in the "oil" of the wise virgins [described in the Gospel of Matthew 25:1–13]). Righteousness is compassion toward man (the spiritual level of a Christian is always inseparable from kindness toward his neighbor). Kindness exists in two forms: one form is the charity which is expressed by generosity; the other is consolation expressed by the words with which one consoles the oppressed. If there is no opportunity to help the unfortunate, then the latter should be assisted by a consoling word. For one consoling word with which you console an unfortunate, you too shall be vouchsafed consolation by the Just Judge with His decisive words at the Last Judgment when He says: "Come, you blessed of My Father, inherit the kingdom prepared for you from the foundation of the world" (Matt 25:34). If you do not comfort the despondent with consoling words, then you yourselves will later hear from the Just Judge these inconsolable words: "Depart from Me, you cursed, into the everlasting fire prepared for the devil and his angels" (Matt 25:41). For charitable love frees man from the anger of God.

Love helps to make a person meek and humble in heart; enmity makes a person violent. Love is always patient and never causes temptation; resentment, however, is always impatient, always causing temptation in a man's heart, so that it never has any peace. Resentment is the mark of the Antichrist, for it imprints upon man's heart the seal of the Antichrist.

What Is the Seal of Antichrist Which Seals Evil People Today, and What Is the Seal with Which Antichrist Will Seal People after His Accession?

Resentment is the mark of the Antichrist and the heart of a spiteful person is sealed with this mark. When the Antichrist (the spirit of the Antichrist acting in the world) places this seal then by this mark of resentment, the heart of man becomes faint (becomes as if dead, incapable of grief for sin, fear of God, or any other spiritual feelings). The saint disclosed the root of the main disturbances of mankind as revolutions, hatred of children for parents, and other discords. These discords are all caused by resentment, or the prideful censure of the shortcomings of our neighbor, disrespect for parents, insubordination to authority, and so forth. If we consider the spirit of the times and the manner of the activities of the enemies of the Church and state, we shall see that they base their whole success chiefly on this, in order to poison people by censure and hatred, and having infected them, to make them their obedient instruments.

When the Antichrist places his seal on people, their hearts will become as if dead. At the time of the prophesied calamity, the Antichrist will begin to seal people with his imprint, as though by this seal to save them from misfortune, for those having this seal, according to the Book of Revelation, will be able to buy bread. Many will be dying on the roads. People will become like predatory birds attacking carrion, and will devour dead bodies. But which people will devour the dead? Those who are marked with the seal of the Antichrist. Since Christians will not have the seal, they will not be able to receive or buy bread and will not devour the dead; but those who are sealed, though they can buy bread, will devour the dead. For, when a man is imprinted with the seal, his heart will become insensitive; not being able to bear hunger, people will carry off corpses, and sitting at the side of any road devour them.

Finally, the one sealed by the Antichrist will himself be put to death; and on the seal the following will be written: "I am yours."—"Yes, you are mine."—"I go of my own free will, not by coercion."—"And I receive you by your own will, not by coercion." These four sayings or inscriptions will be shown in the center of that cursed seal.

Calamities Which Will Overtake the World after the Accession of the Antichrist: The Ocean Will Dry Up, Animals Will Perish, Time Will Accelerate

O, how unfortunate is he who has been sealed with this cursed imprint! This cursed seal will bring a great catastrophe upon the world. For at that time the world will be so oppressed, that people will begin to move from place to place. Then the native population, seeing foreigners, will say: O you unfortunate people! How could you have decided to leave such a grace-filled region as yours, and come to us in our cursed regions, where no human feelings remain with us? This is what will be said wherever people move from one area to another.

Then God, seeing the confusion of the people by which they are evilly distressed, moving to and fro, will command the seas to again become heated as was their former state, so that people would not move from place to place. When the Antichrist occupies his cursed throne, then the sea will boil, just like water boils in a kettle. (This is fully possible in the event of volcanic motion of the sea floor.) When water boils for a time in a kettle, does it not rise as steam? So will it be with the sea. Boiling, it will steam off and will disappear like smoke from the face of the earth.

All growing things on earth will dry up; the groves of trees and bushes will wither from the heat of the sea; the fountains of water will dry up; animals, birds, all creatures will die.

The day will spin like an hour, a week like a day, a month like a week, and a year like a month. For the evil of man will cause even the elements to become strained; they will become tense and hurried, in order that the years of the eighth age, foretold by God, would end more quickly. (This is the eighth millennium from the creation of the world.)

The Sermon of Enoch and Elijah, so That People Receive Not the Seal of Antichrist, but Always Sign Themselves with the Cross; The Slaying of These Preachers

And when the cursed glory of the Antichrist will see Enoch and Elijah preaching and saying to people not to accept the seal of the Antichrist, it will give the order to seize them. They, however, will persuade people not to accept the seal of the Antichrist, and will say that whoever will be patient and will not be sealed by the Antichrist, he will be saved and God will certainly be received in Paradise, if only because he did not accept the seal. Let everyone show the sign of the honorable cross, making its sign at all times, for the sign of the cross frees man from the suffering of hell; but the seal of the Antichrist leads man to the suffering of hell.

If you crave and demand food, bear it a little while, and God, having seen your patience, will send you help from above; you will be revived by aid of the Most High God. If, however, you will not be patient, and will be sealed with the imprint of this foul king, you will later regret this.

People will say to Enoch and Elijah, "Why then are those who received the seal thankful to the Antichrist?" Enoch and Elijah will say: "They are thankful, but who is really thankful? It is not the people who give thanks, only the seal itself." (Malice having triumphed over them, it is expressed through the lips as delight and joy, for it has been successful in defeating these people, as so often happens with robbers, who celebrate and are joyful having completed their crime.)

What is their thankfulness? It is that Satan has entered into them, is conceived in man's feeling, and man does not know what has happened to him. The one who is sealed with the imprint of the Antichrist becomes a demon; even though he asserts that he feels neither hunger nor thirst, he craves food and drink even more, and not only more, but seven times more than you. Be patient for only a little while. Do you not see rather that he who receives the seal of the Antichrist will not live (he is dead in spirit, and eternal suffering awaits him)? Is it possible you too desire to perish with the seal in eternal suffering, there to be with those who were sealed with it?—where there is weeping and gnashing of teeth? Enoch and Elijah will preach to people with many other such exhortations as well.

The Antichrist will hear that two men are preaching, calling him a flatterer, sorcerer, deceiver, and a crafty devil. Hearing of this, he will become angry and order them to be seized and brought to him. With flattering words he will ask them: "What sort of lost sheep are you, that you are not sealed with the king's imprint?" Enoch and Elijah will reply: "Flatterer and deceiver! Demon! It is through your fault that so many souls were destroyed in hell! Most cursed is your seal together with your glory! It is your cursed seal and most defiled glory which have brought the world down to destruction; you have brought the world to a state in which it is expiring and its end has come." The Antichrist will hear such words from Enoch and Elijah and will say to them: "How dare you speak so before me, the autocrat and king?" And Elijah will answer: "We despise your kingdom and curse your glory, together with your seal." The Antichrist will become enraged upon hearing such a scornful answer, and like a mad dog will kill them with his own hands.

After the murder of Enoch and Elijah, the Antichrist will release his most wicked followers (he will free the evil spirits, which he had restrained until now). These offspring or spirits of evil are adultery, fornication, homosexuality, murder, plundering, robbery, lies, tortures, buying and selling of people, and the buying of boys and girls for fornication with them, like unto dogs in the streets. The Antichrist will command these evil spirits who obey him to drive people into doing ten times as much evil as they formerly did; his evil offspring will fulfill this destructive command, striving toward the destruction of man's nature by a diversity of evil doings. From the intensified efforts and great energy of his evil offspring, man's natural feeling and thought will be destroyed.

By their evil deeds these people will surpass demons, and will be of one spirit with them. The Antichrist will see that the nature of man has become more cunning and vain than that of his most evil offspring; he will greatly rejoice that the evil in man has increased, that the natural attributes of man have been lost, and that people have become more evil than demons.

Then the Antichrist, rejoicing at the sight of man's evil, will discover the "double-edged sword" suddenly descending from above, by which he will be slain and his unclean spirit wrenched from his desecrated body. With the death of the Antichrist, murder among people will come to an end. Cain initiated murder and the Antichrist will end it, meaning that with his death it will cease.

CHAPTER TWENTY

The Word of Our Holy Father Ephraim
the Syrian on the Coming of the Antichrist

Is it possible that I, Ephraim,[29] insignificant, sinful, and filled with shortcomings, can be in a position to speak of things that are above my abilities? Yet, inasmuch as the Saviour, in His great goodness taught me wisdom not from books, and in the same way enlightened the faithful everywhere, He will also make my tongue sufficiently clear for the benefit and edification of all who hear, as well as for myself. I begin my talk with pain, and with lamentations I shall speak of the end of the present world, and of that shameless and horrible serpent, who will bring to consternation everything terrestrial, will put fear into people's hearts, faintheartedness, and terrible impiety, and will perform miracles, omens, and terror, "to deceive, if possible, even the elect" (Matt 24:24), and to deceive everybody with false signs and wonders. For it is by the allowance of Holy God that he will receive the power to seduce the world, since the iniquity of the world is fulfilled, and every sort of horror is perpetrated far and wide. Because of the dishonesty of the people, the Most Pure Master will permit the world to be tempted by the spirit of flattery; for people desired to fall away from God and to love the evil one.

It will be a great struggle at that time, brethren, especially for the faithful, when the serpent himself with great authority will perform signs and miracles. When he will show himself like unto God in fearful apparitions, shall fly in the air, and all the demons, like angels, will ascend before the tormentor. For he will cry out with power, changing his appearance and will extremely frighten people. Who then, brethren, will prove to be protected, unshakeable in faith, having in his heart the true sign—the holy coming of the Only-begotten Son, our God. One quickly will see unutterable grief descending on every soul for there will be no comfort or rest from any source at all, neither on earth nor at sea. Soon one will see that the whole world is in confusion, that everyone is hurrying to hide in the hills, that some are dying from hunger, others melt like wax from thirst, and there will be no one to show mercy. Soon one will see that every person sheds tears and asks with longing: "Is the Word of God left anywhere on earth," and hear the answer: "nowhere." Who will endure these days, who will bear the unbearable grief, when he sees the gathering of nations coming from the ends of the earth to see the tormentor, and the many who worship him, calling out in trepidation: "Are you our saviour?" The sea is restless, the earth is drying up, the heavens give no rain, plants wither, and all who live in the east run in great fright towards the west, and those in the west fearfully run to the east. The shameless one, having then taken control, will send his demons to all corners of the earth to boldly proclaim: "The great king has appeared in glory, go and see him." Who then will have such a courageous soul that he might manfully bear all of these temptations? As I have said, where is there such a man, whom all of the angels would glorify?

But I, O Christ-loving and perfect brethren, am terrified at the thought of the serpent, thinking of that grief which will overtake people in those times, and how very cruel to the human race this unclean serpent will prove to be, having even more anger toward the saints who can overcome his illusory miracles. For then there will be found many people who had pleased God and who may be able to be saved in the hills and desert places by many prayers and through ceaseless lamentation. For the Holy God, seeing their indescribable weeping and true faith, will show them mercy, like a tender father, and will watch over them wherever they hide; meanwhile the most evil serpent will continue the search for the saints on earth and at sea, reasoning that since he has already ascended to power all must be subservient to him. Not realizing his weakness and that pride which will cause his fall, the wretch will plot his opposition at that same fearful hour when the Lord will descend from heaven. In the meantime, he will bring the earth into confusion, frightening all by his false, magical signs.

At the time of the serpent's coming, there will be no peace on earth, for it will see great affliction, confusion, bewilderment, death, and hunger everywhere. For our Lord Himself pronounced with His divine lips that such grief has not been seen from the beginning of creation (see Mark 13:19). How shall we sinners then be able to imagine a grief so great, as God described it? Everyone should dwell attentively on the holy pronouncements of the Lord and Saviour, for He, because of extreme need and grief, desires to shorten the time of woe, admonishing us and saying: "And pray that your flight may not be in winter or on the Sabbath" (Matt 24:20); and "Watch therefore, and pray always that you may be counted worthy to escape all these things that will come to pass, and to stand before the Son of Man" (Luke 21:36); for the time is near. All of us are subject to this grief, but do not despair. Worshiping God day and night, let us sinners unceasingly ask in tears and prayer, that we be saved.

Whoever has contrition and tears should entreat the Lord in prayer that he escape from such great grief which will visit the earth, and that he should not see the beast himself, nor the terrors, quakes, hunger, and deaths which will occur all over the world. A steadfast soul is needed in order to be capable of directing one's life amid these temptations. If any person proves to be even slightly careless, he will be more easily captivated and overcome by the signs of the evil and crafty serpent. Such a one will find no pardon at the judgment, for he himself voluntarily believed the tormentor. We shall need many tears and prayers, O beloved, for some of us to firmly withstand these temptations. The beast will produce many visions; for he fights against God, and desires the destruction of everyone.

Listen, O my Christ-loving brethren, to what he did to Israel in the desert, after they had left Egypt; how the evil, vile one, contrived to implicate all in the most grievous sin. He suggested to Balaam the idea of giving to Balak, the Midianite king, the most evil advice of sending the city women out into the huts to capture the Israelites, inclining them to fornication and pagan sacrifices, so that all would act adulterously with these women like dumb animals. God would finally as a result consume all the ungodly. The king set the women up openly before the people, with food at the doors of the huts together with drink-offerings and sacrifices, drawing them unto their death, in order that if they desired to sin with these evil ones, they would first make a drink-offering before entering the hut; for the women accepted nothing from the Israelites, but compelled all coming to them to offer a sacrifice. For the princes he brought out princes' daughters, for the rich, the daughters of the rich, and for the people he brought out many plain women, in order to catch suddenly all in the net of death.

The rich man did not abhor the poor woman or the prince abhor the daughter of some peasant. Observe the work of lies: the evil design! How he dug a pit of destruction unto death for all. Have any one of you ever seen such a shameless affair—fornication armed with a double-edged sword? For the women destroyed those coming to them with a twofold fearful death, inciting them to offer sacrifices, as well as to take part in fornication.

The very same method will be used by the tormentor, in order that all would wear on themselves the imprint of the beast. With the fulfillment of time, he will come to entice all with signs, so that only in this manner they might buy food and necessities for themselves; and for the fulfillment of this decree, he will install leaders. Brethren, turn your attention to the inordinate treachery of the beast, to the artfulness of his evil; he begins with the stomach, so that man, led to extremes by the lack of food, is forced to accept his imprint. This unclean one will have his mark imprinted not on just any part of the body, but so as not to cause difficulty, he will place it on the right hand. He will also place the ungodly imprint on the forehead, so that it would not be possible for a person to use the right hand for making the sign of Christ our Saviour on himself, and without doubt, so that one could not place on his forehead the awe-inspiring and holy name of the Lord and the glorious Cross of the Saviour. For the unfortunate one (the Antichrist) knows, that having the imprint of the Lord's Cross on anyone, will destroy all of his power. Therefore, he will place his sign on the person's right hand, for it is the right hand that makes the sign of the cross on all parts of the body; in the same manner the forehead carries the sign of the Saviour, as the candle stand carries light. So, my brethren, an awesome struggle is in store for all the faithful and staunch Christ-loving people, not to yield even once until the hour of death, and not to succumb when the serpent will begin to imprint his seal in place of the Cross. For he will attempt to use any artifice so that the name of the Lord and Saviour—this Most Holy and Most Pure Name—should never be mentioned. He will do this because of his fear and trepidation at the holy power of the Saviour's name. For whosoever will not be sealed with his imprint, will not be a prisoner of his delusions; the Lord will not renounce such a one, but will enlighten his heart and will attract him to Himself. Tearfully and sorrowfully, I admonish you, the multitude of Christ-loving and faithful servants, that we should not be easily caught by the enemy. Better to say that through the power of the Cross, we should not allow ourselves not to be caught. The inescapable struggle is already at the doors. Let us all accept the shield of faith; let us lovingly draw, from the fountain of God, upon the hope of salvation for our souls. My beloved brethren, I understand the uncreated consubstantial Trinity to be the fountain and source of life. If our souls will be defended by such a weapon, the serpent will be destroyed. At the same time, we should pray that we meet no catastrophes, and not attempt to save ourselves by fleeing in the winter. Therefore, be vigilant as faithful servants who love their Master and are receptive to no other. For this ungodly, threatening thief will come in his time, with the intent of first abducting, slaughtering, and destroying the elect flock of the true Shepherd. He will assume the appearance of a true shepherd in order to beguile the sheep. Those who are well-acquainted with the holy voice of the True Shepherd will immediately recognize the deceiver; for the voice of the ungodly is venomous and does not at all resemble the voice of the True Shepherd. The voice of the thief is feigned, and is soon recognized for what it is. Let us then try to find out in what form the shameless serpent will come on the earth.

The Saviour, intending to save mankind, was born of a virgin, and in the form of a man vanquished the enemy by the holy power of His Godliness; on earth He was meek and humble, in order to raise us up from earth to heaven. This same God, Who truly and actually was conceived, became incarnate, and was born in the flesh of the Holy Virgin, in giving us the commandments saved all by His suffering on the Cross. He will also come again at the last day to judge the living and the dead, and, as a just Judge will reward both the just and the ungodly according to their deeds. The enemy, knowing that the Lord will come from heaven in the glory of His Divinity, therefore intends to imitate the form of His coming in order to seduce all. Our Lord will come to earth in clouds of light similar to fearful lightning. The enemy will not appear on earth in clouds of light, because he is an apostate. For in actuality his instrument will be born of an unclean woman; he will not be incarnate by his own power, but in his image will the devil come, like a thief, in order to seduce all. He will pretend reverence, humility, meekness, and speak of hating falsehood, and turning away from idols, preferring piety, and helping the poor. He will be proper to the greatest degree, very constant, affectionate to all; respecting especially the Jews, for they will be expecting his arrival. Besides all this, he will perform signs, miracles, and instill fear with great power; he will use cunning to please all, so that ordinary people would quickly love him. He will not accept gifts, speak angrily, or show a gloomy expression, but he will always be pleasant. In all of this he will begin to seduce the world by his sedate exterior until he ascends the throne. For when many nations and classes of people will see such good deeds, perfection, and power, all will suddenly conceive the same idea, and with the greatest joy will enthrone him, saying to one another: "How can another such man be found who is so good and truthful?" In the forefront of those glorifying him and rejoicing at his rule will be the Jews and for this reason he will show a preference for them. During the rule on earth of this serpent, the nations will willingly become his allies. Edom, Moab, and also the Ammonites will happily worship him as a legal king, and will be among his first supporters. His reign will be established quickly and he will defeat three great rulers. Then this serpent will become immeasurably exalted in heart and will spew forth his bitterness, discharging lethal poison from Zion. He will dismay the universe, shake it to its ends, oppress it, and defile many souls. He will act now not like a man who is reverent, solicitous, or tender, but at every opportunity grim, cruel, prone to anger, irritable, impetuous, disorderly, dreadful, hideous, hateful, vile, crafty, fierce, destructive, shameless; by his violence he will attempt to drive all mortals to the chasm of ungodliness. He will produce great signs and innumerable catastrophes; but they will all be an illusion, not real events. In a like manner this tormentor will rearrange mountains, but only as a deceitful illusion, and not in reality. In the presence of a huge crowd composed of many nations and classes praising him for his illusory miracles, he will produce a loud sound which will shake the place where the crowds who gather before him stand, and he will proclaim audaciously: "All you nations can now perceive the great power of my rule. Now, before all of you, I command this great mountain standing opposite us that it should move over to us." And the evil one will say: "I command you, immediately to move over to us from across the sea." The mountain will move in the eyes of the onlookers, though not really moving at all from its foundations. For this evil one will not have power over what the Almighty God erected and created from the beginning. He will captivate the world with his magical illusions. Another hill rising from the depths of a great sea, in the form of a large island, will be commanded to leave its place and move to a dry spot on the pleasant shore to please the onlookers. Although the island will not move from the sea at all, it will appear to be a mountain standing on the shore. Then this serpent will stretch out his hands and gather a multitude of crawling things and birds. In like manner he will step out into the deep and walk on it as if on land, presenting this as an illusion, and many will believe, and praise him, as a powerful god. Whosoever has God within him will have illumined eyes of the heart, and with true faith will see and know him rightly. Everyone who has within him the fear of God, and who has illumined eyes of the heart, will know truly that neither the mountain moved from its place, nor did the island move from the sea to the shore.

Then will every soul cry out and groan; then will all see that an unspeakable grief oppresses them day and night, and they will not be able to find food anywhere to appease their hunger. For cruel overseers will be placed everywhere, and only he who has on his forehead or right hand the imprint of the tormentor will be permitted to buy a little food, if any can be found. Then babies will die in their mother's laps, and mothers will die over their children, and a father, with his wife and children, will die in the marketplace, and there will be no one to bury them. Because of the many corpses strewn in the streets, everywhere there will be a foul stench, greatly astounding the living. Amid groaning and nausea, everyone will say in the morning: "When will evening come, so that we can have rest?" When evening comes, they will say to themselves with the most bitter tears: "Will dawn be here soon, so that we may escape the grief which has overtaken us?" There will be no place to run away or hide, for everything will be in confusion on sea and land. This is why the Lord has told to us to be vigilant, urgently praying that you may avoid grief. [See Luke 21:8–28 and 1 Peter 5:8.]

The stench will hang over both sea and land; hunger, earthquakes, confusion, and calamities will abound. The large amounts of gold and silver and silk clothing will not benefit anybody at this time, but all will regard as blessed those dead who were buried before such grief came to the earth. Gold and silver will be scattered over the streets, and no one will touch them for everything has become an abomination. Everyone hurries to run away, yet cannot hide from such grief; instead, together with all the hunger, grief, and fright, they will be gnawed by carnivorous animals and crawling things. Inner fear and outward trepidation; corpses on the streets both day and night. Stench in the haystacks and homes; hunger and thirst, sobbing with rioting everywhere. People greet one another with sobs. Friends and relatives die in the streets while embracing. The beauty of all flesh withers, and people have the look of corpses. The beauty of women becomes loathsome and all flesh and human desire will wither away. However, all who have desires, believed the fierce beast and received his seal—the evil imprint of the profane—will come and say suddenly: "Give us food and drink, for we all waste away suffering from hunger, and keep the poisonous beasts away from us." He, now in trouble and having no means to help, will answer cruelly, saying: "People, how can I give you food and drink? The sky does not want to give water to the earth, and the earth will also not give its harvest or fruits." The people, hearing this, will cry out and shed tears, having no comfort in their grief; instead, another unutterable grief will be added to them, namely, that they believed the tormentor so quickly (that is they will recognize that they were deceived). For since he cannot help himself, how can he comfort them? In those days there will be great deprivation from the many woes caused by the beast, from earthquakes, tumult of the seas, hunger, thirst, and attacks by animals. And all, having accepted the imprint and worship of the Antichrist as a good god, will have no part in the kingdom of Christ, but together with the serpent will be thrown into hell. Blessed is he who at that time is completely holy and faithful, and whose heart is unquestionably devoted to God; for he will fearlessly denounce all of the serpent's proposals, disregarding his tortures and illusions.

Before all this occurs, the Lord in His mercy will send Elijah and Enoch that they might preach true piety to mankind and boldly preach the knowledge of good to all, teaching them not to believe in the tormentor out of fear. They will call out and say: "O people, this is flattery! Let no one believe it and obey the antagonist of God. Let none of you be brought to fright, for he will soon be brought to naught. Soon, the Holy Lord will come from heaven to judge all who have believed His signs." Few will desire to hear and believe this admonition of the prophets.

However, the Saviour will send the prophets in order to show His unutterable love for man; for, even in such times He will not leave mankind without instruction, that all might be without defense at the judgment.

Many of the saints who may then be found at the coming of the foul one shall shed tears to God in rivers, and in order to be saved from the serpent, will hurriedly flee to the deserts. They will hide in the hills and caves in fear, sprinkle earth and ashes on their heads, praying with great humility day and night. This will be granted them by the Holy God. His grace will lead them to specified places, and they will be saved, hidden in chasms and caves, not seeing the frights and signs of the Antichrist; for to those who have knowledge, the coming of the Antichrist will be effortlessly made known. But for whoever has his mind on worldly matters and loves the things of the earth, this will not be clear. For whoever is always tied down to worldly things, even though he hears; he will not believe, and will abhor those who speak. But the saints will be strengthened, for they have cast aside every care for this life.

Then will all the earth and sea cry out, the air, and together with them the wild beasts and the birds of heaven; the hills and crags, and trees on the plains will weep; the heavenly bodies will also weep for mankind. All have turned away from the Holy Lord and believed flattery, having accepted for themselves the mark of the evil, godless one instead of the Life-giving Cross of the Saviour. The earth and sea will weep, for suddenly the chanting of psalms and prayers has ceased from the mouth of mankind; all the churches of Christ will weep greatly, for there will be no church services or divine offerings.

When three and a half years of the rule and deeds of the foul one will have been fulfilled, and all the temptations of the earth will have been completed, then, as foretold, the Lord will finally appear, like lightning flashing in the sky, the holy, most pure, terrifying, and glorious God of all, with incomparable glory. Preceding His great glory will be hosts of angels and archangels, all of them like fiery flames; and the river full of terrible boiling fire; Cherubim with downcast eyes and Seraphim flying and covering their faces with fiery wings and with trepidation calling out: "Arise, you who have died, it is the Bridegroom Who cometh!" The graves will open, and in the twinkling of an eye all of the tribes will be awakened and will look upon the holy greatness of the Bridegroom. Great multitudes of angels and archangels, countless armies, will rejoice with great joy; the saints, the righteous, and all who had not accepted the seal of the ungodly serpent will rejoice. The tormentor, with all of the demons bound by the angels, all who received the seal, all the ungodly and sinners, will be bound and brought to judgment. The King will issue a sentence of eternal condemnation in unquenchable fire. However, all who had not accepted the seal of the Antichrist, and all who had been hiding in caves, will rejoice together with the Bridegroom in the eternal and heavenly mansions with all the saints unto the ages of ages. Amen.

Archimandrite Panteleimon, 1930.

APPENDIX

A Short Biography of Archimandrite Panteleimon (Nizhnik)

Archimandrite Panteleimon was the founder and first abbot of Holy Trinity Monastery, in Jordanville, New York. Father Panteleimon was born Peter Nizhnik on January 16, 1895, in the village of Rechitsa, Grodno Province, Russia. Immigrating to the United States in 1913, he found work in a factory in Chicago. Spurred by the radical changes that were occurring in his homeland due to the Revolution and Civil War, he entered St Tikhon's Monastery in Pennsylvania in 1918. Quickly ordained first a deacon and then a priest, Fr Panteleimon was in charge of agricultural projects at the monastery. Desiring a life even more removed from the vanity and bustle of the world, he wanted to build his own monastery far away in the woods. Along with a fellow desirer of the quiet monastic life Ivan Kolos (the future Archimandrite Joseph), Fr Panteleimon received permission to work in the Sikorsky factory in Connecticut to raise money to buy land for a monastery. Eventually, in 1928 he was able to purchase farmland near Jordanville, New York, where he started to slowly build Holy Trinity Monastery. Facing many early challenges, including a fire that burned down the first wooden church that was built, Fr Panteleimon and his fellow monks nevertheless continued to labor, and eventually were able to build a stone cathedral dedicated to the Holy Trinity, along with a large building to house the monks and printing press. Strengthened with the movement of the St Job of Pochaev Brotherhood from Slovakia, which drew its roots from the famous Pochaev Lavra, the monastery continued the printing tradition of the Pochaev monastery, and became one of the main sources for Russian language spiritual literature and service books during the Soviet period. Father Panteleimon was a tireless compiler and author of spiritual texts. He fell asleep in the Lord in 1984.

Notes

Father Panteleimon was a tireless compiler of Russian language spiritual literature. The references to source material in his original Russian text were to the classic Russian language editions. The author followed a Russian cultural practice where one is not necessarily expected to provide all background detail and source material. Unless otherwise indicated, the quotations and their citations have been translated from the original text.

Chapter Two

1   [*Prayer Book*, Fourth Edition—Revised (Jordanville, NY: Holy Trinity Publications, 2005), p. 27. ISBN 9780884651758.—Ed.]

Chapter Three

2   Orth. Conf., Part 1, answer to questions 64, 65.
3   *Prayer Book.* p. 27.
4   ["May Christ our true God, through the intercessions of His most pure Mother, of our venerable and Godbearing fathers, and of all the saints, have mercy on us and save us, for He is good and the Lover of mankind." *The All-Night Vigil* (Jordanville, NY: Holy Trinity Publications, 2024), p. 65.—Ed.]

Chapter Four

5   [The relics of these saints were hidden until after the collapse of the Soviet Union. The author Archimandrite Panteleimon (1930–46) did not live to see their unveiling.—Ed.]

6   Christian Readings 1885, p. 225.

7   ["Now God worked unusual miracles by the hands of Paul, 12 so that even handkerchiefs or aprons were brought from his body to the sick, and the diseases left them and the evil spirits went out of them" (Acts 19:10–12). —Ed.]

Chapter Five

8   [Tradition says that the Syrian ruler Abgar had leprosy and wrote asking Jesus to come heal him. Jesus wet his own face, wiped it with a towel, creating an image of this face and sent it to Abgar. This is called the Icon of the Savior Not-Made-By-Hands. —Ed.]

Chapter Seven

9   From the works of Bishop Theophan the Recluse.

Chapter Eight

10 From the works of Bishop Ignatius Brianchaninov. [See Ignatius Brianchaninov, *The Field: Cultivating Salvation* (Jordanville, NY: Holy Trinity Publications, 2016).—Ed.]

11 From the works of St Theophan the Recluse.

12 From the 15th instruction of St. Cyril of Jerusalem.

Chapter Nine

13 [St John of Damascus] Book 4, Ch. 7. [See also *An Exposition of the Orthodox Faith*, Book 4, Ch. 26 "Concerning the Antichrist."]

Chapter Ten

14 From the works of Bishop Ignatius Brianchaninov, Vol. 4. [See Ignatius Brianchaninov, *The Field: Cultivating Salvation* (Jordanville, NY: Holy Trinity Publications, 2016).—Ed.]

Chapter Eleven

15 [St John of Damascus] Book 4, Ch. 27.
16 [St Andrew of Caesarea] Explanation of Revelations, Ch. 7.

Chapter Fourteen

17 [St Andrew of Caesarea] Explanation of Revelation; Vol. 13, Ch. 37, p. 62. [Commentary on the Apocalypse]

Chapter Fifteen

18 [St Hippolytus] pp. 129–130.
19 [Blessed Augustine] *The City of God*, Book 20, Ch. 3, pp. 97–98.
20 [St Andrew of Caesarea] 13th word, Explanation of Revelation. [Commentary on the Apocalypse]

Chapter Sixteen

21 [St John Chrysostom] 4th Homily.

Chapter Seventeen

22 ["Let no one deceive you by any means; for that Day will not come unless the falling away comes first, and the man of sin is revealed, the son of perdition, who opposes and exalts himself above all that is called God or that is worshiped, so that he sits as God in the temple of God, showing himself that he is God" (2 Thess 2:3–4) and " The dragon [Satan] gave him his power, his throne, and great authority" (Rev 13:2).]

23 [St Andrew, Archbishop of Caesarea, in his *Commentary on the Apocalypse* says that the capital of the kingdom of the antichrist will be in Jerusalem. See Averky Taushev, *The Epistles and the Apocalypse: Commentary on the Holy Scriptures of the New Testament*, Vol. 3 (Jordanville, NY: Holy Trinity Publications, 2018), p. 300.]

Chapter Eighteen

24 St. Ephraim the Syrian, 105th Homily.

25 Ibid.

26 Ibid.

Chapter Nineteen

27 ["Diligently to seek the Lord; but they shall not find Him, for He has withdrawn Himself from them. For they have forsaken the Lord …" (Hosea 5:6–7); "For the mystery of lawlessness is already at work; only He who now restrains will do so until He is taken out of the way." (2 Thess 2:7)]

28 [This concept (artificial insemination) was entirely new at the time of this revelation which further proves its divine origin.—Translator]

Chapter Twenty

29 [This chapter was compiled by Archimandrite Panteleimon from *The Works of Our Holy Father Ephraim the Syrian.* Part II, III. (in the Russian language).—Ed.]